W9-CAR-381

Home Decorating Solutions

Discover Creative, Fun and Affordable Ideas

CREATIVE
HOME
ARTS
—CLUB—

Creative Home Arts Library™

CREDITS

CREATIVE
HOME
ARTS
—CLUB—

Cover Design, Text and Production: Julie Cisler,
Tom Carpenter, Michele Teigen

Copyright © Creative Publishing international, Inc. 2002

President/CEO: Ken Fund

All information in this book has been tested; however,
because skill levels and conditions vary, the publisher
disclaims any liability for unsatisfactory results. Follow
the manufacturers' instructions for tools and materials
used to complete these projects. The publisher is
not responsible for any injury or damage caused by
the improper use of tools, materials, or information
for this publication.

Printed on American paper by:
R. R. Donnelley
11   / 08

ISBN 1-58923-078-7

CONTENTS

DISCOVER CREATIVE, FUN AND AFFORDABLE *HOME DECORATING SOLUTIONS!*

As a Creative Home Arts Club member, you know how wonderful and rewarding home decorating can be. But you also know the challenges. Where do I get new ideas? How can I add my own creativity and touch? How can I implement the projects both beautifully and affordably?

That's where *Home Decorating Solutions* steps in. These picture-filled pages bring you dozens of decorating ideas that are backed up by specific, step-by-step instructions showing you how to make each project perfectly. There's plenty of room to add your own creative touches too.

You'll start out in "Accessorizing Your Home", with a complete set of lovely and easy projects that can make a big difference in the beauty of your decorating scheme. You'll find everything from twig baskets to decorative picture frames, decoupage art plates to a variety of mosaic accessories you can create.

Move on to "Affordable Decorating", a collection of attractive ideas you can carry out on any budget. Learn new wall design techniques, see how to paint wood floors, discover the magic of enhancing and freshening old and tired furniture, observe how to press flowers and create other botanical delights, and more.

Then we help you do some "Decorating with Great Finds", a chapter that celebrates the value-shopper and pack-rat in all of us. These ideas and instructions show you complete beautiful, useful projects such as: adding a gold-leaf to finish most any old item; turning an old window into a great mirror; creating a tiered tray out of old plates; and building colorful shelves from old shutters.

Finally, step outside with "Decorating the Outdoors", a chapter that helps you make your yard, garden and home's exterior as attractive as the scenery you've created indoors. Discover deck rail planters, trellises, garden stones, bird houses, twig wreaths and much more.

Decorating a home need not be complex, time-consuming, expensive or complicated. With the right ideas and clear instructions—both brought to you via the beauty of full-color photography—you can create projects that will bring joy to both your home and your heart. Let *Home Decorating Solutions* be your guide!

CREATIVE
HOME
ARTS
—CLUB—

ACCESSORIZING YOUR HOME

Accessories are the most personal part of decorating, often giving a room its unique character.

Accessories that have been handcrafted reflect your personality and allow you to customize items to blend with your decorating scheme. Create accessories with heirloom appeal by learning a new craft, such as twig basket weaving or Hardanger embroidery. Or personalize accessories simply by embellishing purchased items, such as baskets, frames and candles.

Baskets, boxes and trays provide decorative accents as well as storage space. Add whimsical painted designs to boxes. Embellish a tray with a tortoiseshell or gilded finish.

Display customized frames and ceramics on tables and shelves. Frames can be embellished to complement your decorating scheme. Clear glass plates become unique decoupage art plates when backed with decorative papers, and plain ceramics become personalized accents when embellished with mosaic tiles.

Any of these accessories can give a fresh look to an older home or add a personal touch to a new one.

TWIG BASKETS

Perfect for a country setting or an eclectic style, these rustic twig baskets are assembled easily using a simple stacking method of construction. Since the baskets are made from gathered twigs, the only purchased materials are the wire nails.

Gather the twigs from a wooded area, looking for twigs that are straight and have a smooth bark. Willow is popular for twig baskets because its high moisture content makes it flexible and prevents it from splitting, but many other woods may also be used. Select twigs with a diameter of ⅜" to ¾" (1 to 2 cm), depending on the desired finished size of the basket. You may gather twigs that have fallen to the ground or cut branches from living trees.

If you plan to have a handle on the basket, you will need to cut that branch from a living tree, selecting one that can be bent into the curved shape without cracking. Plan to use the branch soon after it has been cut to prevent it from drying out.

When nailing two twigs together, select a nail that is no longer than the combined diameter of the two twigs. As you stack the twigs to form the sides, you may use a longer nail, because you will be nailing into the twig below as well as into the two being joined. To prevent the small-diameter nails from bending, support the nail with your thumb and forefinger; this is especially important if you are using hardwood twigs. It is also helpful to tap the nail lightly to avoid bending it.

Twisted handle is made from intertwined, small-diameter branches of dogwood. Each branch of the handle is nailed into the basket twigs.

MATERIALS

- Straight twigs with a smooth bark.
- Wire nails or brads in ⅝", ¾", and 1" (1.5, 2, and 2.5 cm) lengths.
- Hand saw; pruning shears; tack hammer.

Basket with dividers organizes and displays kitchen items. The twig dividers were stacked, row by row, as the basket sides were assembled.

HOW TO MAKE A TWIG BASKET

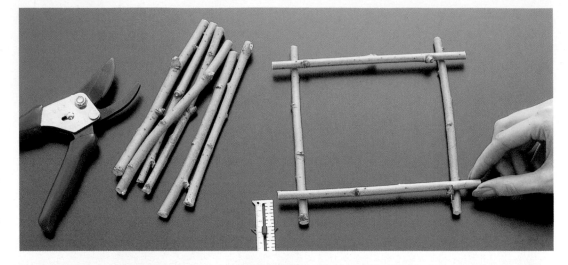

1 Cut twigs to the desired lengths. Lay two twigs on the work surface parallel to each other. Lay two more twigs on top of and perpendicular to the first two; overlap the twigs about 1" (2.5 cm) at corners.

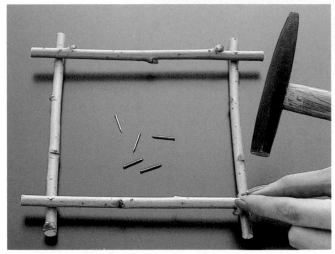

2 Nail the twigs together at intersecting corners, using nails of appropriate length.

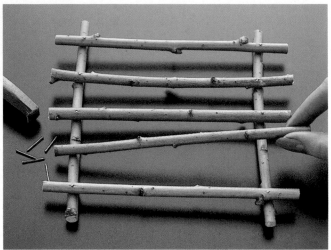

3 Lay twigs for the bottom of the basket perpendicular to first two twigs, spacing them about 1¼" to 1½" (3.2 to 3.8 cm) apart. Nail in place.

4 Lay two twigs perpendicular to the last row of twigs to begin building the sides of the basket. Nail in place at intersections, using 1" (2.5 cm) nails.

5 Add twigs, two at a time, laying them perpendicular to each previous row; nail in place, using 1" (2.5 cm) nails. Continue until the desired height is reached.

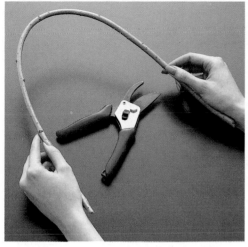

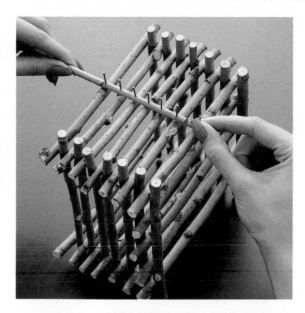

2 Place handle on center of one side of basket, with cut end of branch even with bottom of the basket. Press nails of appropriate length into handle where it intersects twigs of basket.

1 Cut branch to desired length for handle. Bend the branch to determine in which direction it bends more easily.

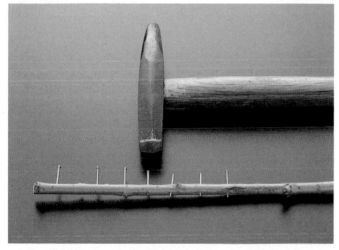

3 Lay handle on sturdy work surface; drive nails through the diameter of the handle.

4 Reposition the handle on the basket; nail in place.

5 Bend the handle to the other side of the basket. Repeat steps 2 to 4.

6 Nail the handle again through each twig (arrow), from the inside of the basket, using side of hammer, if necessary.

DECORATING
BASKETS

Add your personal touch to purchased baskets by topping them lavishly with ivy or garland, then adding embellishments, such as latex fruit or silk flowers.

For a more rustic look, encircle a basket with bundles of wheat, and tie it with raffia. Or trim the rim of the basket with moss, fallen birch bark, and other dried naturals. For a romantic touch, simply weave a fancy ribbon into an open-weave basket.

Baskets with lids can be made into decorative accessories that provide hidden storage space. Top the lid with silk flowers or preserved leaves. Or embellish the lid with items that reflect a hobby, such as beach-combed seashells, sewing notions, or fishing tackle.

Most items can be secured to baskets using a hot glue gun and glue sticks. For temporary placement, you can secure items with wire or floral adhesive clay.

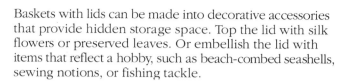

Moss trims the rim of a basket, with a fanciful bird's nest used as an accent.

Ivy tops this birch basket and twists around the handle. The clusters of latex berries complete the arrangement.

Woven ribbon adds a simple but elegant touch to an open-weave metal basket.

Dried naturals, including pods and preserved leaves, add interest to the lid of the basket at right.

Wheat stems, bundled together, encircle a basket (opposite). Raffia adds a touch of country.

HOW TO MAKE AN IVY-TOPPED BASKET

MATERIALS

- Basket.
- Silk ivy vines or artificial garland.
- Embellishments, such as latex fruit or silk flowers.
- Wire and wire cutter; or hot glue gun and glue sticks.

1 Cut several vines of ivy or a length of artificial garland, and arrange around top of basket; secure with wire or hot glue.

2 Twist ivy around handle of basket, if desired; secure with wire or hot glue. Arrange and secure latex fruit or silk flowers.

HOW TO MAKE A WHEAT-STEM BASKET

MATERIALS

- Wheat with long stems.
- Rubber bands.
- Raffia.
- Old scissors.
- Hot glue gun and glue sticks.

1 Cut several wheat stems to desired lengths, using old scissors. Group stems in bundles; secure with rubber bands.

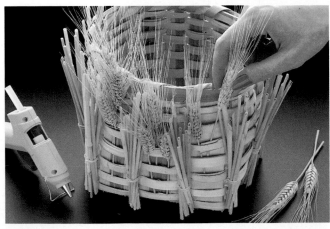

2 Secure bundles to sides of basket, using hot glue. Add heads of wheat, tucking stem ends into or between the bundles.

3 Tie a length of raffia around the basket, concealing rubber bands.

HOW TO MAKE A MOSS-RIMMED BASKET

MATERIALS

- Moss.
- Embellishments, such as lichens, fallen birch bark, twigs, and other dried naturals; small craft bird's nest, optional.
- Hot glue gun and glue sticks.

1 Secure pieces of moss to basket rim, using hot glue, applying it to both the inside and the outside of rim.

2 Glue lichens and other dried naturals to moss, scattering them around the rim. Glue bird's nest in place, if desired.

HOW TO EMBELLISH A BASKET WITH WOVEN RIBBON

MATERIALS

- Open-weave basket.
- Ribbon and bow.
- Large-eyed needle.
- Wire, for securing bow.

1 Thread ribbon into a large-eyed needle. Weave ribbon in and out of the basket.

2 Wire bow to one side of basket, concealing ends of woven ribbon.

HOW TO EMBELLISH A BASKET WITH A LID

MATERIALS

- Basket with lid.
- Embellishments, such as dried seed pods, stones, and preserved leaves.
- Hot glue gun and glue sticks.

1 Arrange dominant or larger embellishments on lid of basket as desired. Secure with hot glue. Some items can be used as a base for smaller items to add height to the arrangement.

2 Add secondary or smaller embellishments, stacking items as desired.

TROMPE L'OEIL BOXES

Decoratively painted wooden boxes can accent desks, countertops, and end tables as well as provide needed storage for small items. Designs painted in trompe l'œil, which means "fool the eye," add whimsy to simple wooden boxes. On the following pages, the instructions and any necessary patterns are given for three designs with a trompe l'œil effect. Choose either a box tied with a ribbon bow, a wrapped parcel, or a stationery box.

Use unfinished wooden boxes with hinges, available at craft stores in a variety of sizes. Or decorate boxes found at garage sales or gift shops. If you choose an unfinished box, sand it as necessary, and use a primer before applying the base coat of paint. If painting a box with a varnished surface, lightly sand the surfaces to ensure good paint adhesion.

Use good-quality brushes to achieve even edges and fine lines. Test the paints for proper consistency; a detailed design is often easier to achieve with slightly thinned paints.

To protect the painted finish on the box, apply an aerosol acrylic sealer, available in matte and gloss finishes. A matte finish is recommended for the parcel box; either a matte or a gloss finish is appropriate for the bow and stationery boxes.

MATERIALS

- Wooden box.
- Graphite paper.
- Acrylic paints.
- Artist brushes, such as a flat shader and a liner.
- Fine permanent-ink pen.
- Stationery, to use as pattern guide for stationery box.
- Aerosol acrylic sealer.

Trompe l'œil designs (below) are painted on wooden boxes to create a stationery box, a wrapped parcel, and a box tied with a ribbon bow.

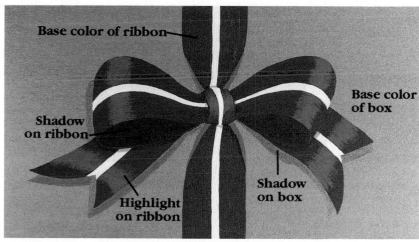

Highlights and shadows add a dimensional effect to painted designs. To paint the highlights, mix white paint with the design's base color. For example, add highlights to a red bow by mixing white paint with red. To paint the shadows, use a darker shade of the base color or mix black with the base color. For example, use a darker red for the shadows inside the loop of the bow; use a darker brown for the shadows that are on top of the box.

HOW TO PAINT A BOW BOX

1 Apply base coats of paint; allow to dry. Transfer bow design (page 21) to top of box, using graphite paper.

2 Tape box closed at ends. Using pencil, lightly mark ribbon placement by extending lines from bow, 1⅛" (2.8 cm) wide, along top, front, and back of box. For stripes of ribbon, mark lines ½" (1.3 cm) from ribbon placement lines.

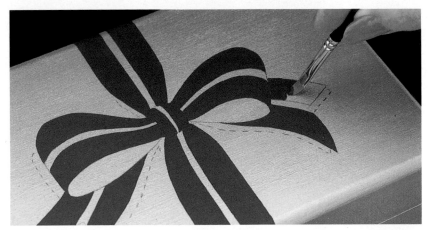

3 Paint outer stripes of ribbon using artist's brush, such as a flat shader. Allow paint to dry.

4 Paint the center stripe of the ribbon; allow to dry.

5 Mix a lighter shade of the colors used for the ribbon, using white paint. Highlight the ribbon as shown, to add dimension.

6 Paint a shadow effect on the ribbon as shown, using a darker shade of the ribbon color and thinning the paint for a translucent effect. Paint shadow effect on box as shown, using a darker shade of box color and thinning the paint. Apply aerosol acrylic sealer, if desired.

HOW TO PAINT A PARCEL BOX

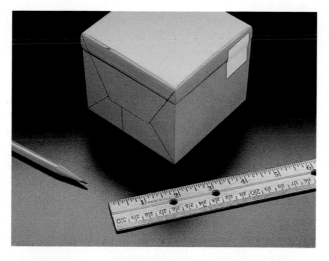

1 Apply base coats of paint; allow to dry. Tape box closed. Using pencil, lightly mark fold lines of paper as shown, on opposite sides of box.

2 Mark placement for string along sides and top of box, drawing knot at center of box top.

3 Paint fold lines of paper, using darker shade of box color; do not paint where string will overlap fold lines. Allow to dry. Paint highlights and shadows as shown.

4 Apply white paint along marked lines for string; allow to dry. Paint highlights and shadows on one side of string; paint the center knot detail.

5 Mark area for the postage stamp; transfer stamp design (page 21) using graphite paper.

6 Paint stamp, using thinned paint. When dry, paint the lettering and price on stamp, using a permanent-ink pen.

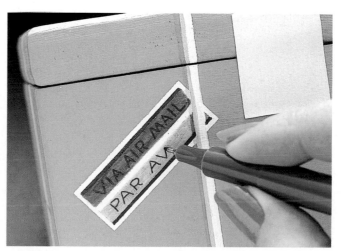

7 Transfer and paint additional labels (page 21) on box, taking care not to paint over the string. Apply aerosol acrylic sealer, if desired.

HOW TO PAINT A STATIONERY BOX

1 Paint or stain box; allow to dry. Mark lines for belt, 1" the (2.5 cm) apart and centered on box, around the top, front, and back. Paint belt, using brown paint; allow paint to dry. Transfer belt details, key, and eyeglasses (opposite) onto box, using graphite paper. Mark placement of eyeglass chain. Mark ¼" (6 mm) strips around the box at lower edge of the top and 1" (2.5 cm) from lower edge of box.

2 Paint the strips around the box, using black paint. Paint the buckle, key, and eyeglasses, using gold paint; for eyeglass chain, use wooden end of brush to paint dots. Paint highlights and shadows of items as shown.

3 Complete belt details, and paint ribbon for key. Paint highlights and shadows as shown.

4 Tape stationery to the top of the box; trace to mark placement. Mark ¼" (6 mm) border on top of box, 1" (2.5 cm) from edges.

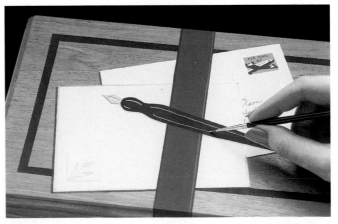

5 Paint and outline the stationery. Paint postage stamp as on page 19, steps 5 and 6. Write address on envelope, using permanent-ink marking pen.

6 Transfer fountain pen and stationery design (opposite). Paint border on top of box, fountain pen, and stationery design, using black and gold paints. Paint shadows and highlights. Apply aerosol acrylic sealer, if desired.

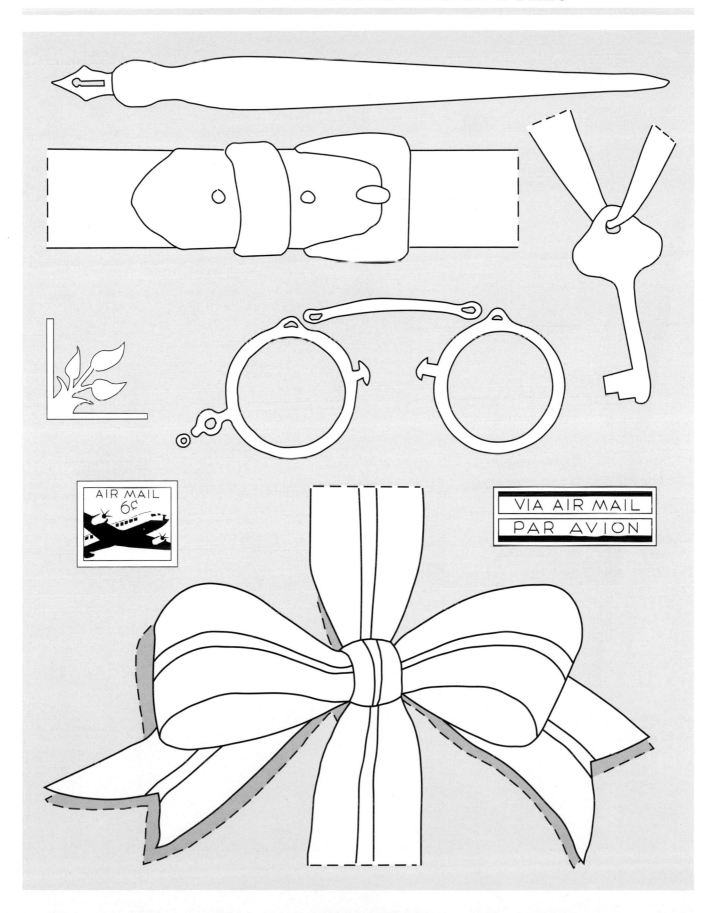

AIR MAIL
6¢

VIA AIR MAIL
PAR AVION

DECORATIVE TRAYS

Turn plain trays into stunning accessories by applying a decorative finish. Choose from simplified gilding or a tortoiseshell finish.

Oil-based paints, such as Japan paints, are used for both techniques. Japan paints, available in small containers, are sold at art supply stores and with stenciling supplies at many paint stores.

Gilded designs are applied using precut Mylar® stencils and metallic powder. Apply the metallic powder over a surface of tacky varnish. The result is a stenciled surface that is much smoother and more subtle than that achieved by stenciling with metallic paints. Metallic powders are available at art supply stores in a wide range of colors, from silvery white to rich bronze gold.

A tortoiseshell finish is achieved by streaking thinned varnish stains over a painted base. An orange-red paint, often called barn red, is used for the base coat, and varnish stains in dark oak and black are used for the streaking. The dark oak varnish stain is available at paint and hardware stores, and the black is created by adding black artist's oil color.

Select a tray with smooth, flat surfaces, lightly sanding any prevarnished surfaces to ensure paint adhesion. It is easiest to apply a tortoiseshell finish to a flat, horizontal surface. For this reason, paint the sides of the tray in a solid color and apply the tortoiseshell finish to the bottom only; tape off the sides before working on the bottom of the tray.

Purchased trays *can have a painted tortoiseshell finish, as shown above. Or they can be decorated with a stenciled gilded design and then varnished, as shown opposite.*

HOW TO GILD A TRAY

MATERIALS

- Oil-based paint, such as Japan paint, for base coat.
- Oil-based clear varnish, in gloss or semigloss finish.
- Metallic powder in desired color.
- Precut Mylar® stencil.
- Masking tape.
- Scrap of velvet or chamois leather.

1 Apply a base coat of oil-based paint to a clean, prepared surface; allow to dry. Apply a coat of varnish. Allow varnish to dry about 3 to 5 hours, until slightly tacky; at this time, if the corner of stencil is pressed against the varnish, stencil can be removed with a slight pull, but will leave no mark.

2 Pour a small amount of metallic powder into a bowl. Position stencil in desired location; cover surrounding area on tray by taping paper to stencil.

3 Wrap a scrap of velvet or chamois leather around index finger, wrapping it smoothly so there are no wrinkles or creases at fingertip. Dip wrapped finger into metallic powder; rub on a piece of paper to remove excess powder.

4 Gently rub area to be gilded, starting at the center and working out. As necessary, pick up more powder and reposition stencil. Remove stencil, and allow varnish to dry at least 24 hours.

5 Remove any powder outside design area by rubbing gently with mild abrasive cleanser. Wash the surface gently, using soapy water. Rinse and dry.

6 Seal the gilding by applying a coat of varnish; allow varnish to dry.

HOW TO APPLY A TORTOISESHELL FINISH TO A TRAY

MATERIALS

- Oil-based paints, such as Japan paints, in orange-red and black.
- Dark oak varnish stain, in gloss finish.
- Black artist's oil color in small tube.
- Mineral spirits.
- Two flat 2" (5 cm) paintbrushes; round artist's brush.
- Oil-based clear varnish, in gloss or semigloss finish, optional.
- Masking tape.

1 Apply black paint to sides of tray; allow to dry. Tape off inside lower edge of tray sides, using masking tape.

2 Apply base coat of orange-red paint to bottom of tray; allow to dry. Squeeze a small amount of black oil color into a bowl; dilute with dark oak varnish stain until mixture will flow, and set aside to be used in step 5.

3 Dilute dark oak varnish stain, about one part mineral spirits to two parts varnish; apply over base coat of paint, using flat paintbrush.

HOW TO APPLY A TORTOISESHELL FINISH TO A TRAY

4 Brush irregular, diagonal zigzag strokes across the surface of the wet varnish.

5 Apply diluted black oil color from step 2 in irregular streaks, parallel to diagonal brush strokes and about 2" (5 cm) apart; use a pointed artist's brush and a sideways rolling motion. Allow the surface to harden for 1 to 2 minutes.

6 Stroke the bristle tips of a clean, dry paintbrush gently over the black streaks, in the same direction as they were painted; this will give wispy edges.

7 Repeat step 6, stroking in opposite diagonal direction; this merges some of the streaks. Repeat as necessary to even up the design, taking care not to darken all of the base color.

8 Allow surface to dry. For a more durable finish, apply a coat of clear varnish to bottom and sides of the tray.

MORE IDEAS FOR DECORATIVE TRAYS

Blonde tortoiseshell finish is achieved by applying a base coat of metallic gold paint, followed by a dark oak varnish. Artist's oil colors in burnt umber and black are used for the streaked effect.

Gilded tray with two colors of metallic powder is achieved by using a stencil kit that contains a separate stencil plate for each metallic color.

HARDANGER EMBROIDERY

Hardanger embroidery, with its geometric designs, blends well with most decorating schemes. Hardanger designs are easy to follow and to adapt. Most designs can be stitched by following a close-up photograph.

The embroidery is worked on 22-count Hardanger fabric. This basket-weave fabric is composed of a pattern of squares; each square is made of two strands. Traditionally, pieces were stitched on white fabric with white thread; however, variations combine different colors of fabric and thread.

Learning a few basic Hardanger stitch patterns enables you to create a variety of pieces. You may want to practice the stitches on a small sample before you begin a project. The Hardanger embroidery shown here illustrates various stitch patterns. The finished piece measures 8½" (21.8 cm) square, a suitable size for a first project.

The satin-stitch block is the primary stitch pattern; each block consists of five stitches over four fabric squares. The blocks can be stitched in a variety of patterns, such as a staircase effect or motifs with cutwork. The buttonhole stitch, a variation of the satin-stitch block, forms the edging for many projects. The star motif is also a satin-stitch block variation. Cutwork blocks are stitched using wrapping and web stitches. Satin-stitch blocks, buttonhole stitches, and star motifs are worked using #5 pearl cotton and a size 22 tapestry needle. Work the wrapping and web stitches for cutwork blocks using #8 pearl cotton and a size 24 tapestry needle.

MATERIALS

- 22-count cotton Hardanger fabric.
- Pearl cotton, #5 and #8.
- Tapestry needles, sizes 22 and 24.
- Sharp, fine-pointed scissors.

TIPS FOR WORKING HARDANGER EMBROIDERY

Practice the stitches, using a contrasting thread, before starting a project.

Check your work often to make sure blocks are properly aligned with the weave of the fabric.

Leave 3" (7.5 cm) thread tails, securing them by weaving the ends under completed stitches on the wrong side of the piece.

Clip threads, rather than carry them; the wrong side of the piece should appear as neat as the right side.

Cut fabric for cutwork by cutting only on the side where the stitches have entered the fabric; never cut parallel to a satin-stitch block.

*Hardanger stitch patterns include cutwork motifs **(a)**, satin-stitch blocks **(b)**, star motifs **(c)**, and buttonhole stitches **(d)**. The stitches are worked counting the fabric squares, according to a close up photograph.*

1 Cut one 12" (30.5 cm) square of fabric, folding it in quarters to find center of fabric; finger-press. Stitch the center motif of satin-stitch blocks (opposite), starting at a corner about 2½" (6.5 cm) from the center.

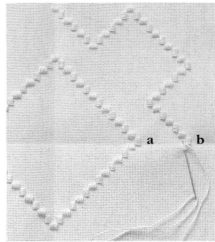

2 Stitch the outer satin-stitch block design; there are 28 squares between the corner block of the center motif **(a)** and the corresponding block of the outer design **(b).** Check work frequently to see that blocks are correctly aligned with the weave of the fabric.

3 Finish design by stitching the outer row of buttonhole stitches, opposite.

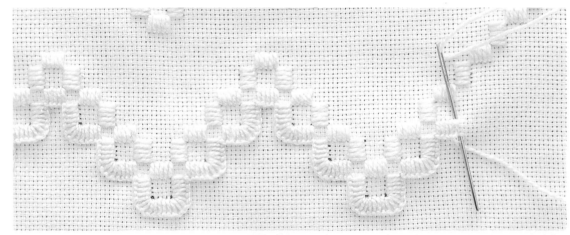

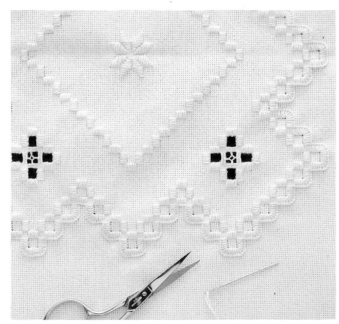

4 Stitch the center star motif (page 33). Stitch cutwork motifs (page 32), using wrapping stitch; add web stitch to center of each cutwork block, if desired.

5 Finish the edges of the hardanger project as on page 33.

HOW TO MAKE SATIN-STITCH BLOCKS

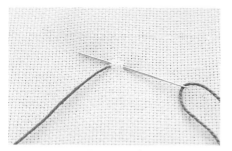

1 Bring needle up and count over four squares; insert the needle, bringing the needle out one square above where thread entered fabric.

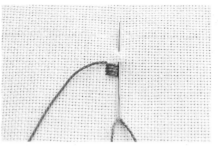

2 Stitch to complete first five-stitch block; on fifth stitch, pivot needle and bring needle up four squares away.

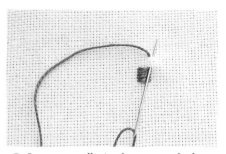

3 Insert needle in the corner hole of previous block to make first stitch of second block.

4 Complete five stitches for the second block; turn second corner by bringing needle up in same hole as last stitch.

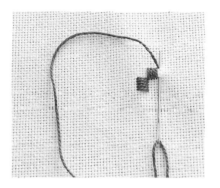

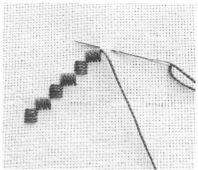

5 Repeat from step 1 for the desired number of satin-stitch blocks, turning corners for desired design.

HOW TO MAKE BUTTONHOLE STITCHES

1 Bring needle up four squares from satin-stitch block. Insert at corner of block and bring out at thread entry, with thread looped under needle. Stitch four additional parallel stitches, looping thread under needle each time.

2 Stitch three diagonal stitches, using the corner hole of the fifth parallel stitch for each diagonal stitch; this forms rounded, outside corner.

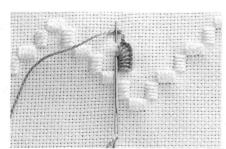

3 Stitch the first parallel stitch of the second block, using the same corner hole.

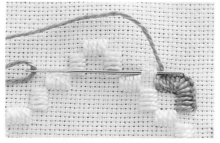

4 Stitch five stitches of second block; at completion of fifth stitch, pivot needle, and stitch across four squares, bringing it up in corner hole of the fifth stitch; this will become the inside corner.

5 Repeat from step 1 for desired number of buttonhole stitches, turning outside and inside corners for desired design. When you run out of thread, start using a new length of thread at an inside corner.

HOW TO MAKE A CUTWORK MOTIF

1 **Wrapping stitch.** Stitch a motif of 12 satin-stitch blocks. Carefully cut the fabric as shown; fabric is cut only on the side where the stitches have entered the fabric, never parallel to a satin-stitch block.

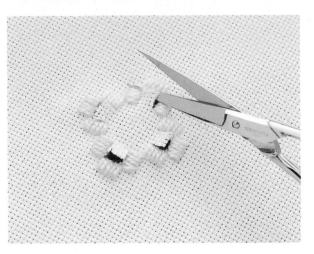

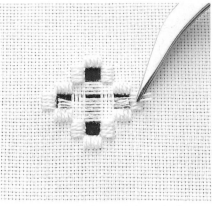

2 Remove all clipped threads from the fabric.

3 Secure thread on wrong side of fabric, and bring needle up through middle of the four unwoven fabric threads. Bring needle around one side and up through the middle.

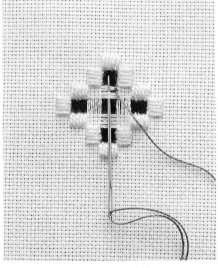

4 Bring needle around the opposite side and up through the middle.

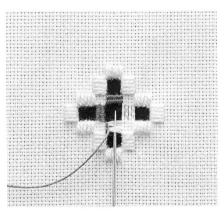

5 Continue wrapping thread in a figure-eight pattern, pulling each stitch tightly. At completion of first bar, bring needle up through middle of next bar, and repeat to wrap all four sides; if web is desired, wrap one-half of the fourth side.

1 **Web stitch.** Follow steps 1 to 5, above, wrapping one-half of the fourth side; insert needle up through center of adjacent bar, creating first web section.

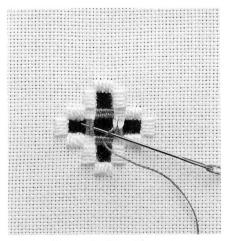

2 Insert needle under web section, then up into next bar.

3 Repeat at third bar. Complete the web by bringing needle over and around first web section. Insert needle up into center of uncompleted bar; finish wrapping the bar.

HOW TO MAKE A STAR MOTIF

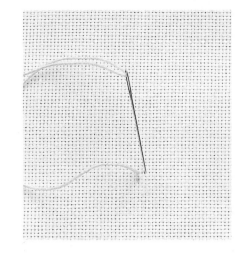

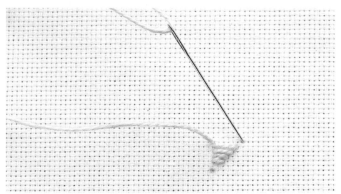

1 Locate center hole for star (as indicated by dot), and count up two squares; bring needle up. Work first satin stitch over two squares.

2 Stitch four additional stitches, increasing the length of each stitch on the right side by one square; fifth stitch covers six squares.

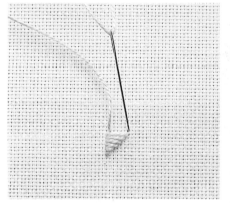

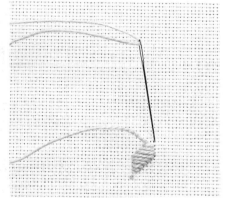

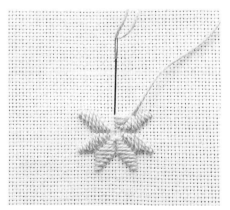

3 Work next stitch by decreasing length on left side by one stitch; stitch remains parallel with previous stitch on the right side.

4 Stitch three additional stitches, decreasing the length of each stitch on left side by one square; ninth stitch covers two squares.

5 Insert needle under stitches on wrong side; continue to make eight spokes, working from center out, adjoining spokes share holes. Star is worked in mirror-image pairs.

HOW TO FINISH THE EDGES OF A HARDANGER PROJECT

1 Machine-stitch around the border of the design, stitching just inside the ridge of the buttonhole stitch; use short stitch length and lightweight matching thread. (Contrasting thread was used to show detail.)

2 Trim as close as possible to buttonhole edge, using sharp scissors and taking care not to clip the pearl cotton thread.

MORE IDEAS FOR HARDANGER EMBROIDERY

Placemat, *adapted from an heirloom Hardanger design, is worked on a 16" × 20" (40.5 × 51 cm) rectangle of fabric; the finished size is 12¼" × 16" (31.2 × 40.5 cm). The design consists of satin-stitch blocks, buttonhole stitches, and half-star motifs. Cutwork has been done on the inner satin-stitch blocks, as on page 32. Work the design, counting squares in the fabric and the stitches in the actual-size photograph below.*

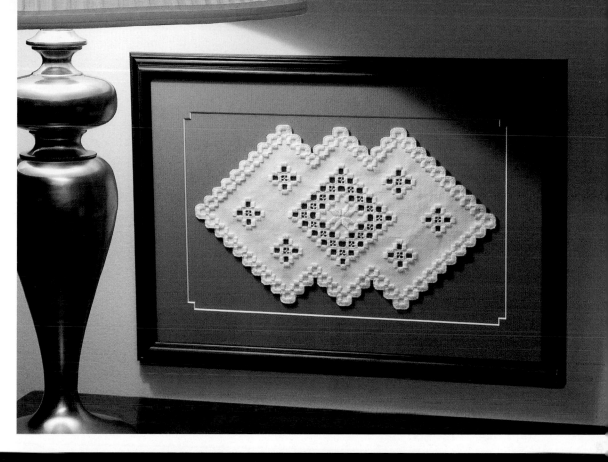

Framed doily is mounted on a dark background to highlight the cutwork. Worked on an 11" × 15" (28 × 38 cm) rectangle of fabric, the finished size is 7½" × 11½" (19.3 × 29.3 cm). The design consists of satin-stitch blocks, buttonhole stitches, and cutwork and star motifs. Work the design, counting the fabric squares and stitches in the actual-size photograph below.

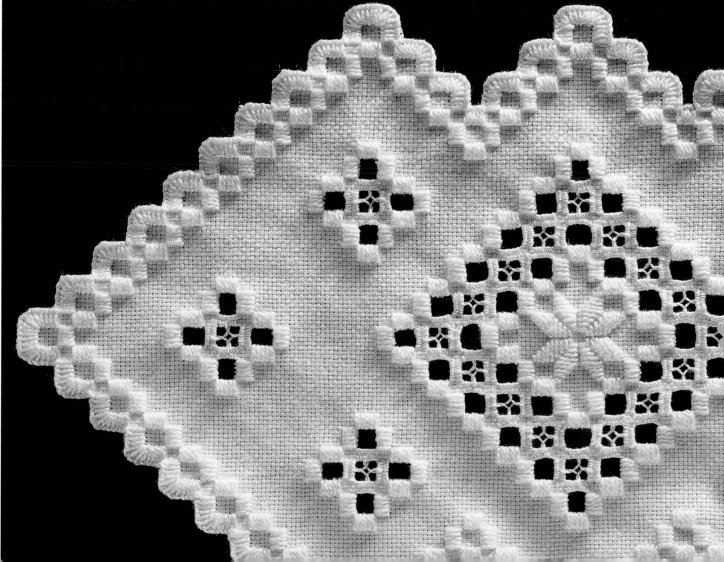

DECORATIVE FRAMES

Starting with simple frames for pictures or mirrors, you can create frames that are eye-catching conversation pieces. A mix of several frames in various styles can be grouped together for added impact.

For a rustic, woodland look, make twig frames (top left). Or use your creativity to add moss, stones, or other natural materials (pages 40 and 41).

Embellished frames (far left) are quick and easy to make. Any number of items can be glued to frames, including buttons, coins, gemstones, beads, or charms.

Use a glue that will bond to both the frame and the embellishment. Hot glue is suitable for many items, including plastics, twigs, and bark. When gluing metal items, use a glue suitable for metals, such as a jewelry glue. When applying moss, use a wood glue. Because there must be sufficient bonding surface between the frame and the embellishment, a frame with a flat surface usually works best.

Decoupage frames (near left), embellished with cutouts from gift-wrapping paper, can be made in designs from Victorian to whimsical. Prepare the cutout motifs, following the instructions for art plates on page 42. For a quick decoupage finish, use an aerosol glaze. For a thick gloss on frames, use a glaze formulated for a triple-thick, extra-thick, or deep-gloss finish.

HOW TO MAKE A TWIG FRAME

MATERIALS

- Frame with flat surface in a color that matches the twigs.
- Straight twigs that will fit closely together.
- Hot glue gun and glue sticks; utility scissors.

1 Plan twig placement; cut twigs to the desired lengths. Position twigs on frame, arranging them as necessary for a close fit.

2 Secure twigs to one side of frame, applying the hot glue to the twigs. Glue twigs starting at inner edge of frame and working toward outer edge. Continue securing twigs to complete all sides.

HOW TO MAKE AN EMBELLISHED FRAME

MATERIALS

- Frame.
- Wire cutter.
- Embellishments, such as charms, shells, beads, buttons, and coins.
- Glue, appropriate for securing embellishments.

1 Remove any unnecessary hardware, such as button shanks or charm loops, from embellishments, using a wire cutter.

2 Plan placement of the items; for visual interest, consider using an asymmetrical design or extending some items over edge of frame.

3 Secure items with glue; to avoid excess glue, apply it sparingly to back of charm, making sure to cover all flat surfaces that will be in contact with frame.

HOW TO MAKE A DECOUPAGE FRAME

MATERIALS

- Frame.
- Gift-wrapping paper.
- Decoupage medium.
- Small sponge applicator, optional.

- Scissors with fine, sharp blades and points; curved cuticle scissors, for intricate, curved motifs.
- Spray glaze.

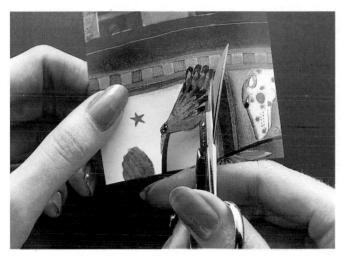

1 Cut out desired motifs from wrapping paper; if using cuticle scissors, cut with curved blades of scissors away from the motif.

2 Plan the placement of the motifs. Apply a thin layer of decoupage medium to back of motif, using sponge applicator or finger; secure to frame, taking care not to tear paper. Wipe any excess decoupage medium from frame.

3 Secure other embellishments, such as faceted stones, taking care not to use excessive amount of decoupage medium; allow to dry overnight.

4 Elevate frame on a piece of scrap wood or a jar. Apply several coats of spray glaze, allowing the glaze to dry between coats.

MORE IDEAS
FOR DECORATIVE FRAMES

Spanish moss and twigs *embellish a mirror with a simple, wide frame.*

Bundled twigs, *tied with raffia, make a woodland frame.*

***Buttons
and beads***
*are tied at
the corner
of a rustic
frame. A
hole drilled
through the
frame allows
for lacing the
items.*

Polished stones *are glued to a frame to complement a nature print.*

Gift card *is cut to make a decorative mat. Use a straightedge and a mat knife to cut an opening for the picture.*

DECOUPAGE ART PLATES

Transform a clear glass plate into a unique decorative plate, using simple decoupage techniques and motifs cut from gift-wrapping paper. The motifs are glued to the back of the plate with a decoupage medium. For a background with a dimensional effect, paints are then applied, using a sponging technique. Varnish is applied as a sealer over the sponged paint.

For the motifs, select high-quality gift-wrapping papers, often sold in individual sheets; avoid papers that are very light in weight. Designs from greeting cards and antique reproduction prints may also be used for motifs. For best results when working with heavy papers such as greeting cards, reduce the thickness by peeling away one or more layers.

MATERIALS

- Clear glass plate.
- Gift-wrapping paper.
- Decoupage medium; brush or sponge applicator.
- Acrylic paints; small piece of natural sea sponge, for applying paints.
- Scissors with fine, sharp blades and points.
- Curved cuticle scissors, for intricate, curved motifs.
- Aerosol acrylic sealer.
- Sponge or brayer.

HOW TO MAKE A DECOUPAGE ART PLATE

1 Cut out the desired motifs from gift-wrapping paper; if using cuticle scissors, cut with curved blades away from motif.

2 Outline paper motifs or highlight the designs, using marking pens, if desired. Seal the ink with aerosol acrylic sealer.

3 Trace the plate on piece of paper; plan placement of motifs. Clean the back of plate thoroughly, using glass cleaner and lint-free rag; place plate face down on table.

4 Apply a thin layer of decoupage medium to the front of center foreground motif, using sponge applicator or finger.

5 Position the motif on back of plate; smooth out bubbles or wrinkles, using a dampened sponge or brayer. Any excess decoupage medium around edges of the motif will not show when the plate is painted.

6 Continue applying motifs, working out from center of plate; if motifs are layered, work from foreground to background. Allow decoupage medium to dry.

7 Apply thin coat of decoupage medium to the back of the motifs as a sealer; allow to dry.

8 Apply the lightest color of acrylic paint, using natural sea sponge; apply sparingly.

9 Apply remaining layers of paint, finishing with darkest color. If desired, paint back of plate a solid color, using an aerosol acrylic paint.

10 Personalize plate with signature and date, using permanent-ink marking pen.

11 Apply light coat of aerosol acrylic sealer; allow sealer to dry. Apply second coat.

MOSAIC
ACCESSORIES

The art of mosaic transforms a utilitarian vase into a dramatic piece of artwork. Made from broken or cut tiles separated by sanded grout, each mosaic piece has a unique quality. Tiles can be applied over any surface that is clean, dry, and structurally sound. If the surface is glossy, lightly sand it before applying the tiles.

Ceramic tiles, available in matte and gloss finishes, may be cut into squares or rectangles no smaller than ¾" (2 cm), or into random shapes, then applied to a vase, clay pot, or other accessory. Large tiles are sold individually, and smaller tiles may be purchased in sheets that cover about 1 sq. ft. (30.5 sq. cm); tiles in sheets may be pulled off the mesh backing.

The ceramic tiles are cut into the desired shapes and sizes with a tile cutter. The surface of the tile is first scored with the tool's cutting wheel. Then the tile is broken along the scored line by pressing the breaking wings of the cutter against the tile.

Several types of tile cutters are available. A hand cutter may be used for cutting the softer tiles. With this cutter, you will need to measure the cutting lines and mark them on the tile with a marking pen; the markings can be wiped off with a dampened rag after the tile is cut.

For tiles that are so hard they cannot be cut successfully with a hand cutter, use a large commercial-type cutter, which may be borrowed or rented from a tile store. The commercial-type cutter is more convenient for cutting tiles into exact dimensions without having to mark the cutting lines. Set the guide on the cutter for the desired dimension; then lay the tile on the cutter against the guide. You will still need a hand cutter to break the tiles, because the breaking wings on a commercial-type cutter are too wide to break the small pieces necessary for making mosaic designs.

To cut random-shaped pieces of tile, use the breaking wings of a hand cutter without scoring the tile. Grip the tile against the breaking wings, and squeeze firmly. When using a hand cutter, you may want to break the tiles inside a paper bag, as a safety precaution and to help keep the work area clean.

Plan the mosaic design before beginning. Measure the space on the vase or pot to determine the size of the tiles to be cut. If you want to work in rows, determine the number of rows that will fit, planning to space the tiles ⅛" to ¼" (3 to 6 mm) apart. Keep in mind that the spacing between the tiles does not have to be exact; some irregularity adds to the unique character of the piece.

Tile cutters include a commercial-type cutter **(a)** for cutting hard tiles and a hand cutter **(b)** for cutting softer tiles.

MATERIALS

- Vase, clay pot, or other accessory.
- Ceramic tiles in matte or gloss finish; shards of pottery may be substituted.
- Ceramic adhesive or multipurpose household adhesive, such as Liquid Nails®.
- Tile cutter.
- Sanded tile grout and grout float.
- Plastic ice-cream bucket; rubber gloves.
- Cellulose sponge.
- Coarse nylon sponge.
- Self-adhesive felt pad, for bottom of vase or pot.
- Grout sealer, optional.

HOW TO MAKE A MOSAIC VASE

1 Set the guide on commercial-type tile cutter to desired width. If using a hand cutter, mark cutting line on tile. Score tile with cutting wheel by pulling wheel firmly and slowly across tile.

2 Break tile along the scored line with a hand cutter, centering scored line between breaking wings. Press with slow, steady motion.

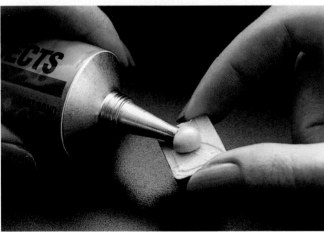

3 Squeeze a pea-size bead of adhesive onto the wrong side of the tile.

4 Press the tile onto the clay vase or pot in the desired location, beginning with narrowest portion of vase or pot. For faster setting, pull tile away from vase; air dry for 5 to 8 minutes.

5 Continue applying tiles as in step 4. Allow adhesive to cure for 16 to 24 hours, until the tiles have firmly set.

6 Prepare the sanded grout according to the manufacturer's directions.

7 Apply grout by drawing grout float across tiles at a slight angle to the surface, forcing the grout into spaces between tiles; wear rubber gloves. Use the short side of the grout float for small projects, the longer side for large projects. Go over each area two or three times, making sure grout is worked in thoroughly, filling in all gaps and air holes.

8 Remove the excess grout from tiles, using a dampened cellulose sponge, after about 20 minutes or when grout is firm, but not completely hardened; rub dampened sponge in circular motion over tiles.

9 Rub the tiles with a coarse nylon sponge to remove the haze, 2 or 3 hours after the first cleaning was done with dampened cellulose sponge.

10 Paint inside of vase, or any areas not covered with mosaic, with grout that has been diluted with water to a thin consistency. Polish the tiles with a clean, dry cloth. Apply grout sealer, if desired.

Mosaic tabletop transforms this small table into a unique accent piece. Apply the tiles to an existing tabletop or to a top cut from plywood.

Plaster pedestal *is decorated with tiles. The scrollwork areas of the pedestal are painted with sanded grout that has been thinned with water.*

Shallow bowl *is created by covering a terra-cotta saucer with mosaic tiles inside and out.*

Shards of pottery *have been substituted for tiles, for a more irregular piece of artwork.*

The warm glow of candles makes a room inviting. A wide array of candles is available, from slender tapers to chunky pillars.

For a romantic touch, use delicate French ribbon to add bows and streamers to candles. Or secure embellishments to a chimney-style candle with floral adhesive or rubber bands, which are then concealed with ribbon or raffia.

Candles can be quickly embellished with decorative nail heads. To avoid excessive cracking, use nail heads with prongs not longer than ⅛" (3 mm) and press the prongs gently into the candle.

Clusters of candles *create a simple centerpiece with impact. Opposite, the pillar candles are enhanced with French ribbons and studded with decorative nail heads.*

Chimney-style candles *can be surrounded by sprigs of holly and evergreen. Or twigs can be tied around the chimney with raffia.*

Floating candles *and smooth glass stones in a clear, heavy dish suggest the tranquility of a woodland pool.*

AFFORDABLE DECORATING

Decorate your home at a reasonable cost and with great style.

As a do-it-yourselfer, you can give your home a new look without spending a lot of money. Make your own furnishings or adapt what you already have in a creative, fresh approach to home decorating.

Furniture can represent the largest portion of the budget. To save money, buy unfinished furniture in basic styles, then enhance the pieces with medallions, moldings, pierced tin panels, cutouts or resist-stain stenciling.

Floors and walls offer a creative opportunity with decorative painting—an inexpensive way to dramatically change a room. Paint a wood floor to achieve a high-end designer look. Or paint a sisal rug to create a customized area rug. For the walls, use a decorative painting technique such as block printing or scumbling, instead of using an expensive wallcovering.

Complete the decorating scheme with accessories that look great, making sun catchers, framed botanicals and decorative boxes, all at a fraction of the cost of purchased ones.

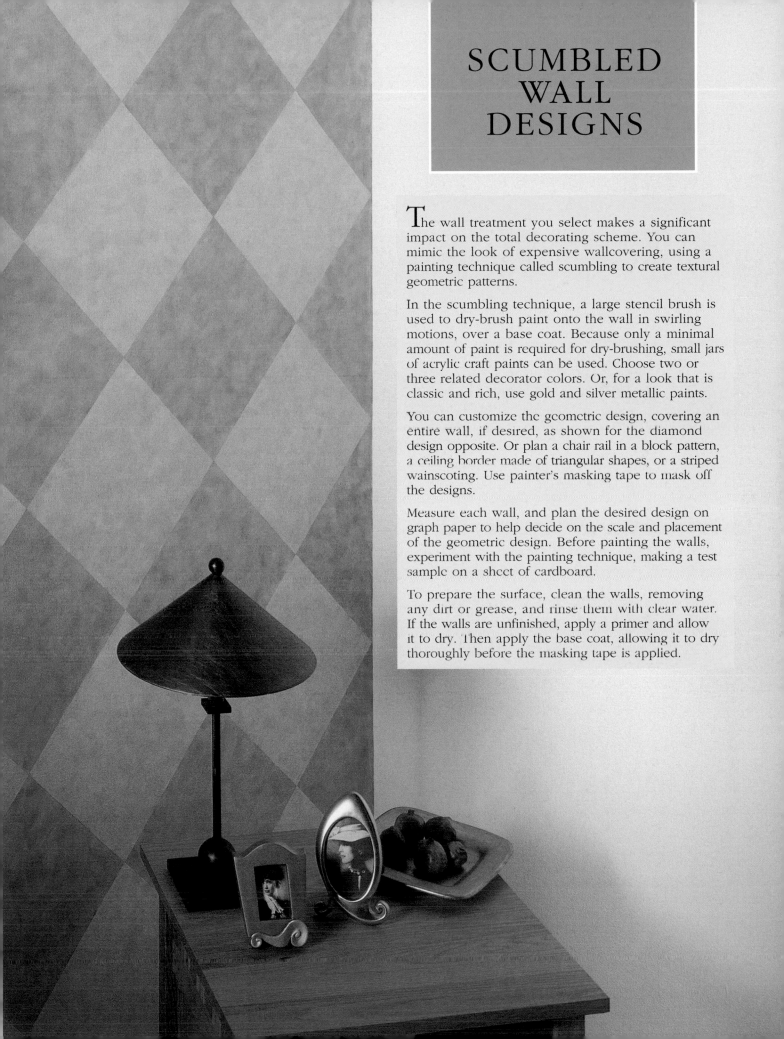

SCUMBLED WALL DESIGNS

The wall treatment you select makes a significant impact on the total decorating scheme. You can mimic the look of expensive wallcovering, using a painting technique called scumbling to create textural geometric patterns.

In the scumbling technique, a large stencil brush is used to dry-brush paint onto the wall in swirling motions, over a base coat. Because only a minimal amount of paint is required for dry-brushing, small jars of acrylic craft paints can be used. Choose two or three related decorator colors. Or, for a look that is classic and rich, use gold and silver metallic paints.

You can customize the geometric design, covering an entire wall, if desired, as shown for the diamond design opposite. Or plan a chair rail in a block pattern, a ceiling border made of triangular shapes, or a striped wainscoting. Use painter's masking tape to mask off the designs.

Measure each wall, and plan the desired design on graph paper to help decide on the scale and placement of the geometric design. Before painting the walls, experiment with the painting technique, making a test sample on a sheet of cardboard.

To prepare the surface, clean the walls, removing any dirt or grease, and rinse them with clear water. If the walls are unfinished, apply a primer and allow it to dry. Then apply the base coat, allowing it to dry thoroughly before the masking tape is applied.

HOW TO PAINT A SCUMBLED WALL DESIGN

MATERIALS

- Painter's masking tape.
- Wide-blade putty knife.
- Carpenter's level; straightedge.
- Latex or craft acrylic paint, for base coat.

- Latex or craft acrylic paints in desired colors, for scumbling.
- Stencil brush, 1" (2.5 cm) in diameter.
- Disposable plate; paper towels.

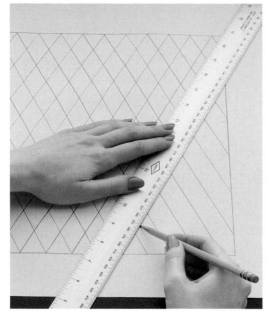

1 Measure the wall. Plan the design to scale on graph paper.

2 Apply base coat of paint, using paint roller; allow to dry thoroughly. Draw design on wall in light pencil markings, using carpenter's level and straightedge.

3 Indicate which areas are to be masked off, using small pieces of masking tape. Apply painter's masking tape to marked areas; use a putty knife to trim the masking tape diagonally at corners as shown. Press firmly along all edges of tape, using plastic credit card or your fingernail to seal tightly.

4 Pour a small amount of each paint color onto disposable plate. Dip the tip of the stencil brush into first color. Using a circular motion, blot brush onto folded paper towel until the bristles are almost dry.

5 Wrap fingers around handle of brush as if to make a fist. Brush paint onto the wall in vigorous, wide, circular motions, working in a small area at a time and changing the direction of the circular motions frequently; overlap the paint onto the masking tape. Build up the color to desired intensity, but allow base coat to show through. Use all of the paint on bristles.

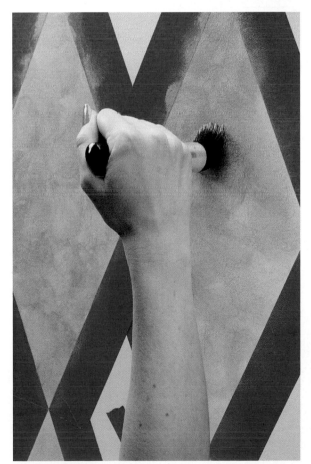

6 Dip the stencil brush into the second color; blot. Apply the paint randomly over the same area, building up color to varying intensities throughout the area. Repeat with a third color, if desired.

7 Repeat the technique to complete the entire wall, working in one small area at a time and blending areas together. Remove masking tape when paint is dry.

BLOCK-PRINTED WALLS

Block printing is a simple stamping technique that can be used to apply repeated motifs to walls. In this technique, paint is applied to a printing block of wood and foam, then stamped onto the surface to be painted. The block prints can be aligned to form a border, arranged in a set pattern, or scattered randomly.

Closed-cell foam, available at art supply stores and hardware stores, works especially well for making printing blocks, because it cuts easily. Applied to a wood block for easier handling, the closed-cell foam has the necessary flexibility to make clean prints, even on somewhat irregular wall surfaces.

Closed-cell foam is manufactured in several forms. Thin foam sheets with pressure-sensitive backing can be purchased at art supply stores. These are easily cut with scissors into the desired shapes. Another closed-cell foam is neoprene, a synthetic rubber manufactured for use as an insulator. It is commonly available for use as weather stripping in a pressure-sensitive tape, ⅜" (1 cm) thick; however, in this form, the widest tape available is ¾" (2 cm). Neoprene can also be purchased in sheet form, through suppliers listed in the Yellow Pages under Foam. A computer mouse pad made of neoprene can also be used, although the surface may be textured.

Use acrylic craft paints for block printing on walls. Make a stamp pad for transferring the paint to the printing block by soaking a piece of felt with the paint. A small amount of paint extender increases the open time of the paint, keeping the stamp pad moist longer. It is a good idea to practice with the printing block on paper before printing on the wall, to become familiar with the placement of the design in relation to the outer edge of the block.

MATERIALS

- Closed-cell foam, available as thin, pressure-sensitive sheets, pressure-sensitive tape, neoprene sheets, and computer mouse pads.
- Wood block, cut slightly larger than design.
- Acrylic craft paints; acrylic paint extender.
- Felt; sheet of glass or acrylic.
- Craft glue, if foam is not pressure-sensitive.

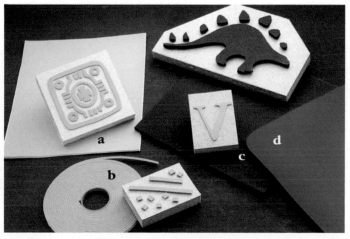

Printing blocks are made from closed-cell foam cut to the desired shapes and attached to a wood block. Closed-cell foam is available as thin, pressure-sensitive sheets **(a)**, neoprene weather-stripping tape **(b)**, neoprene sheets **(c)**, and computer mouse pads **(d)**.

HOW TO MAKE THE PRINTING BLOCK

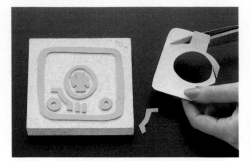

1 Cut tracing paper to same size as the wood block; make pattern for design on tracing paper. Mark top of design on pattern and on edge of block. Transfer design onto the back of the closed-cell foam **(a),** using graphite paper. Transfer the mirror image of design on underside of wood block **(b).**

2 Cut the foam on design lines, using scissors. Peel paper from pressure-sensitive backing; affix to the wood block, following the transferred design lines. If using foam without pressure-sensitive backing, affix foam to wood block with craft glue.

3 Glue the original pattern on opposite side of the block, taking care to position it in the same direction as the design on the underside.

HOW TO BLOCK-PRINT THE DESIGN ON A WALL

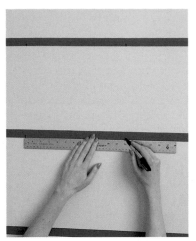

1 Mark placement for design motifs on wall, using masking tape or light pencil line.

2 Thin the paint slightly with an acrylic paint extender, about three to four parts paint to one part extender. Cut a piece of felt, larger than printing block; place felt pad on glass or acrylic sheet. Pour the paint mixture onto felt, allowing paint to saturate pad.

3 Press printing block into felt pad, coating surface of foam evenly with paint.

4 Press the printing block to the wall at placement mark, applying firm, even pressure to back of block. Remove the block by pulling it straight back from the wall.

5 Repeat steps 3 and 4 for each block print. Add paint to the felt pad as needed. Touch up any poor impressions, if desired, using a small brush, sponge, or piece of foam.

MORE IDEAS FOR BLOCK PRINTING

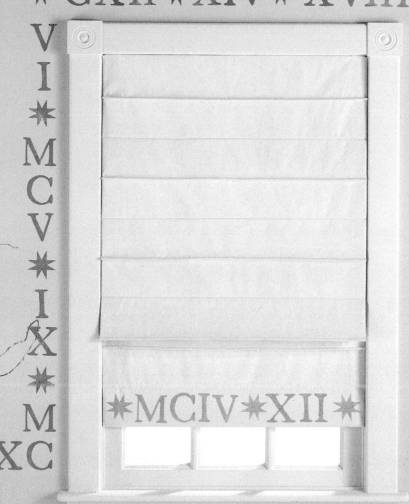

Block-printed border on this stitched-tuck Roman shade matches the border on the wall. To block-print on the fabric, mix two parts of acrylic paint with one part of textile medium, rather than use an extender. In making the shade, omit the bottom row of rings so the printed border shows when the shade is raised.

Two-color border is created using a separate block for each color and section of the design.

Dinosaurs are block-printed randomly across the walls of a child's bedroom.

DECORATING
SISAL RUGS

Sisal rugs are inexpensive and durable floor coverings with a classic look. As an alternative to either wool or synthetic area rugs, sisal rugs can work well with any decorating style. Customize a sisal rug with decorative painting, or apply a contrasting fabric border around the rug, repeating one of the fabrics used for other room furnishings.

The term *sisal* includes true sisal as well as similar plant fibers, such as coir, jute, rice, sea grass, and maize. True sisal, coir, and jute are coarse fibers and can be rough in texture. The fibers used to make rice, sea grass, and maize

rugs are smoother in texture and less abrasive to bare feet. All of the plant fibers can be woven into various patterns, including squares, diamonds, herringbones, and chevrons.

For painted designs, select a rug made from coarse fibers, because the paint adheres better to a porous surface. Use acrylic or latex paints, applying the paint with a stencil brush. Designs that are medium-to-large in scale work best, due to the rough texture of the rug. Mask off areas to be left unpainted, or use a stencil to paint design motifs.

For fabric borders, use a mediumweight to heavyweight fabric, such as canvas or duck, affixing the fabric to the rug with hot glue. The border may be any desired width, but a 3" to 5" (7.5 to 12.5 cm) finished width makes a striking framed edge without covering up too much of the sisal.

Before painting or applying a border to a sisal rug or placing furniture on it, unroll the floor covering and let the fibers relax at least 24 hours. Sisal can be placed directly on bare wood, vinyl flooring, or concrete, but you may want to place a nonslip pad under the rug for safety.

Sisal *is a family of plant fibers that includes: (top row, left to right) true sisal, maize, and sea grass; (bottom row, left to right) rice, jute, and coir. All of these plant fibers can be woven into a variety of patterns.*

HOW TO PAINT BORDERS OR STRIPES ON A SISAL RUG

MATERIALS

- Rug of porous plant fibers, such as true sisal, coir, or jute.
- Acrylic or latex paints.
- Painter's masking tape.
- Stencil brush.
- Aerosol clear acrylic sealer.

1 Mask off borders and stripes with painter's masking tape, pressing it firmly to the rug; follow woven rows in the rug whenever possible.

2 Apply paint, using a stencil brush in an up-and-down motion and working the paint into the fibers of the rug. Allow to dry.

3 Remove painter's masking tape. Apply aerosol clear acrylic sealer to painted area of rug.

HOW TO PAINT A STENCILED DESIGN ON A SISAL RUG

MATERIALS

- Rug of porous plant fibers, such as true sisal, coir, or jute.
- Acrylic or latex paints.
- Stencil plates; stencil brush.
- Painter's masking tape.
- Aerosol clear acrylic sealer.

1 Plan placement for design on entire rug before painting. It may be helpful to position photocopies of stencil plate on rug to visualize the design and plan the spacing.

2 Tape stencil plate to rug. Apply paint, using a stencil brush in an up-and-down motion and working the paint into the fibers of the rug. Allow to dry. Apply aerosol clear acrylic sealer to painted area of rug.

HOW TO APPLY A FABRIC BORDER TO A SISAL RUG

MATERIALS

- Plant-fiber rug.
- Mediumweight to heavyweight fabric.
- Hot glue gun and glue sticks.

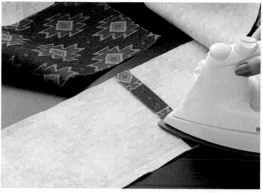

1 Cut strips of the border fabric, with the cut width equal to twice the desired finished width of the border plus 1" (2.5 cm). Seam the strips together as necessary for a combined length equal to the perimeter of the rug plus 3" to 4" (7.5 to 10 cm). Press seams open.

2 Press seamed border strip in half lengthwise, wrong sides together. Press under ½" (1.3 cm) on both long edges of strip.

3 Wrap border strip over edge of the rug, beginning at one corner, so outer fold is centered on the edge; extend the end about 1" (2.5 cm) beyond the corner.

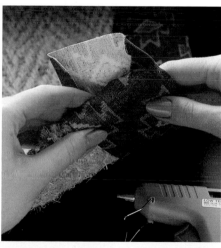

4 Fold under extended end of border strip as shown, encasing the outer edge of the rug; secure with hot glue.

5 Secure the border strip to top side of rug at the inner folded edge, applying glue 3" to 4" (7.5 to 10 cm) at a time; use an ample amount of glue. Press border strip firmly in place; work quickly before glue sets.

6 Fold the border strip diagonally at corner to form miter; glue in place. Continue gluing along the next side of the rug.

7 Fold the end of strip diagonally at the last corner to form miter; trim off excess fabric. Glue in place.

8 Turn rug over, and repeat steps 5 to 7 on the underside of the rug.

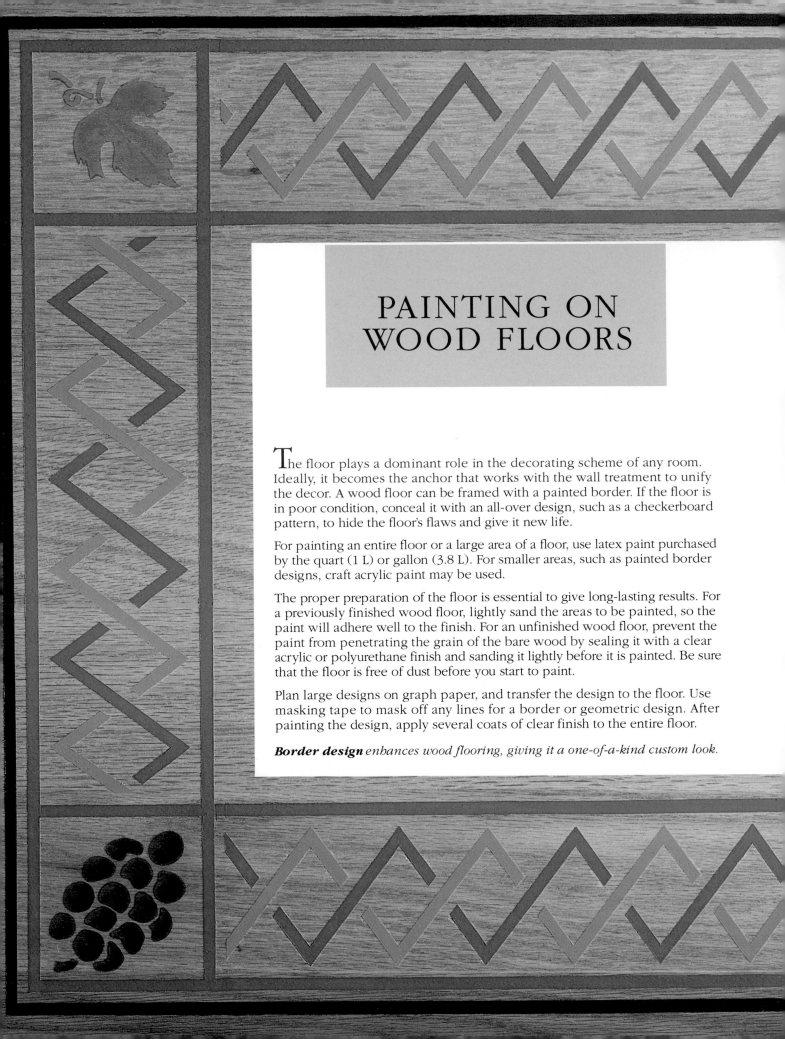

PAINTING ON WOOD FLOORS

The floor plays a dominant role in the decorating scheme of any room. Ideally, it becomes the anchor that works with the wall treatment to unify the decor. A wood floor can be framed with a painted border. If the floor is in poor condition, conceal it with an all-over design, such as a checkerboard pattern, to hide the floor's flaws and give it new life.

For painting an entire floor or a large area of a floor, use latex paint purchased by the quart (1 L) or gallon (3.8 L). For smaller areas, such as painted border designs, craft acrylic paint may be used.

The proper preparation of the floor is essential to give long-lasting results. For a previously finished wood floor, lightly sand the areas to be painted, so the paint will adhere well to the finish. For an unfinished wood floor, prevent the paint from penetrating the grain of the bare wood by sealing it with a clear acrylic or polyurethane finish and sanding it lightly before it is painted. Be sure that the floor is free of dust before you start to paint.

Plan large designs on graph paper, and transfer the design to the floor. Use masking tape to mask off any lines for a border or geometric design. After painting the design, apply several coats of clear finish to the entire floor.

Border design *enhances wood flooring, giving it a one-of-a-kind custom look.*

Checkerboard design *has a classic look that works with any decorating scheme, depending on the colors selected.*

- Graph paper.
- Tape measure; straightedge.
- Fine sandpaper.
- Tack cloth.

- Painter's masking tape.
- Latex or acrylic paint.
- Paintbrushes.

- Materials listed on page 21, for block-printed border design.
- High-gloss and satin clear finishes, such as acrylic or polyurethane.

HOW TO PAINT AN ALL-OVER CHECKERBOARD DESIGN ON A WOOD FLOOR

1 Sand the surface of previously stained and sealed wood floor lightly, using fine sandpaper, to degloss the finish; this improves paint adhesion. Vacuum the entire floor, and wipe with tack cloth.

2 Mask off baseboards with painter's masking tape. Paint the entire floor with the lighter of the two paint colors. Allow to dry thoroughly.

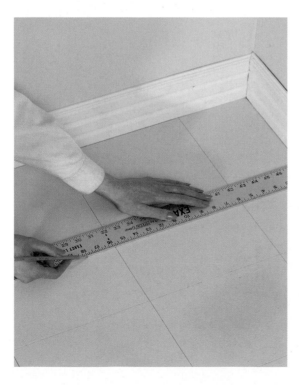

3 Measure the floor. Decide on the size of squares to be used. Plan the design so that areas of the floor with the highest visibility, such as the main entrance, have full squares; place partial squares along opposite walls. Mark design lines on the floor, using a straightedge and a pencil.

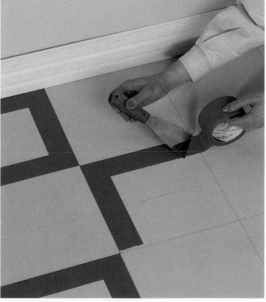

4 Mask off squares that are to remain light in color, using painter's masking tape, as on page 58, step 3.

5 Paint the remaining squares with the darker paint color. Remove the masking tape from squares carefully before paint is completely dry.

6 Apply a coat of high-gloss clear finish, using sponge applicator; allow to dry. Sand lightly with a fine sandpaper. Wipe with tack cloth. Apply two coats of satin clear finish.

HOW TO PAINT A STRIPED & BLOCK-PRINTED BORDER DESIGN ON A WOOD FLOOR

1 Sand the surface of previously stained and sealed wood floor lightly in the area to be painted, using fine sandpaper, to degloss the finish; this improves the paint adhesion. Vacuum entire floor, and wipe with tack cloth.

2 Mark design lines for border on floor. Mask off stripes in design, if any, using painter's masking tape; press firmly along edges with a plastic credit card or your fingernail, to prevent the paint from seeping under the tape.

3 Apply paint for the stripes, using a paintbrush. Remove masking tape. Allow paint to dry.

4 Block-print the designs as on pages 61 and 62. Seal entire floor with clear finish as in step 6, above.

MORE IDEAS FOR PAINTED FLOORS

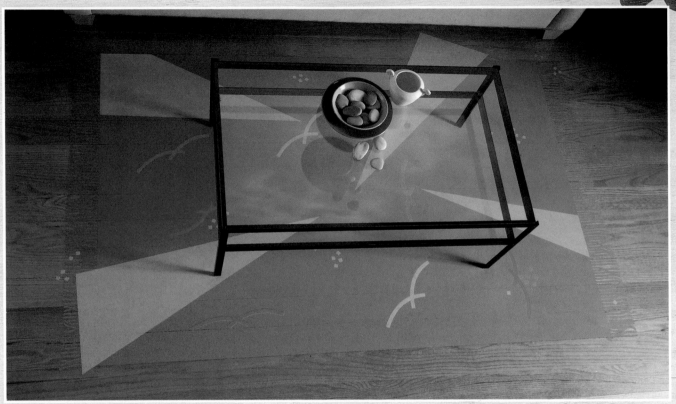

Faux area rug, *painted on the floor area under a coffee table, becomes a whimsical accessory.*

Checkers game board *is painted on the wood floor in a corner of the family room. Mock box floor pillows are used for comfortable seating while playing checkers.*

Stenciled design (above) is painted on a whitewashed wood floor, using precut stencils and a stencil brush.

Hopscotch is painted on a concrete game-room floor. To prepare the concrete floor, wash it with muriatic acid solution, following the manufacturer's instructions. Then paint it, using floor-and-deck enamel. It is not necessary to seal the floor-and-deck paint with a clear finish.

ENHANCING BASIC FURNITURE

For attractive, yet economical, furniture, purchase unfinished pieces, and paint or stain them yourself. Furniture in basic styles is the most reasonably priced and can be changed in various ways for the look of more expensive, detailed pieces.

Pierced tin panels can be added to door fronts for an authentic country look. Resist-stain stenciling creates the look of inlaid wood at a fraction of the cost, and wood medallions can be added to mimic traditional

Basic unfinished furniture can be changed in a number of ways, for the look of an expensive piece at a fraction of the cost.

wood carvings. Decorative wood moldings can add the finishing touch to furniture.

When shopping for unfinished furniture, look for good quality in construction. Choose wood that will accept the desired stain well. This may require some experimenting on scrap wood of the same type before making a final purchase. Sand the furniture completely and wipe the surface free of dust, using a tack cloth, before staining or painting the furniture piece.

Medallions accent the doors and drawer of this painted armoire.

Pierced metal panels (page 76) are added to the recessed areas of these cabinet doors.

Decorative wood moldings add subtle detailing at the top of this armoire and above the drawer.

Wood panel cutouts *add dimensional detailing to these cabinet doors.*

Resist stain stenciling *on this cabinet creates a contrasting design.*

PIERCED METAL PANELS

Achieve an authentic country look by adding pierced metal panels to cabinet doors, trimming the panels with a narrow wood molding. On a flat-surfaced door, create a panel by mounting the pierced metal panel in the center of the door, edged with a wood molding. If the cabinet has recessed panels, mount the metal panels in the recessed area. Some cabinet doors have a removable center panel that can be replaced with the pierced metal panel.

For the pierced metal, purchase precut medium-gauge tin or copper sheets at craft stores in sizes ranging from 5" × 7" (12.5 × 18 cm) to 12" × 18" (30.5 × 46 cm). Other metals that can be used are thin-gauged galvanized sheet metal and hobby aluminum.

The necessary equipment for piercing the metal is minimal and inexpensive. Punching tools, awls, and engravers (shown opposite) can be purchased at craft stores in a choice of sizes. Although best results are achieved by using piercing tools, nails of various sizes and sharpened screwdrivers or chisels can be substituted.

Prepare the work surface by placing a piece of plywood over a cushion of newspaper, using a new piece of plywood for each panel that you pierce. To pierce the holes, strike the piercing tool with a mallet or hammer. Before beginning the project, experiment on a scrap of metal to determine how hard to hit the piercing tool in order to create the desired hole size, practicing the technique until you are able to pierce holes that are consistant in size.

You may purchase patterns for the pierced design. Or create your own pattern, using a simple line drawing or quilting stencil. Make a separate copy of the pattern for each panel you are piercing, saving the original. A new pattern is used for each panel so it is easy to see which holes have already been punched.

Piercing tools are available in several styles. Punching tools **(a)**, used to punch copper and other lightweight metals, have sharpened points and slim wooden handles. Awls **(b)**, used to punch holes in tin and other heavy metals, have sharpened metal points and knob-shaped wooden handles. Engravers **(c)** and chisels **(d)** have sharp chiseled ends for piercing short lines.

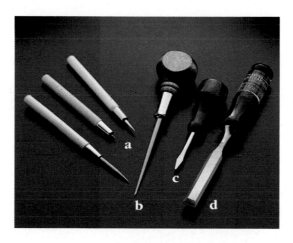

MATERIALS

- Medium-gauge tin or copper sheets, thin-gauge galvanized sheet metal, or hobby aluminum.
- Piercing tools or nails and sharpened screwdriver.
- Pattern and tracing paper.
- Scrap of plywood.
- Wide duct tape.
- Tin snips.
- Fine steel wool.
- Newspaper.

HOW TO MAKE PIERCED METAL PANELS

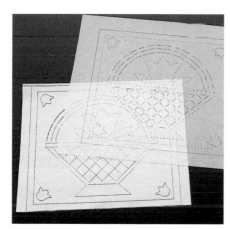

1 Cover the drawing with tracing paper; copy the lines, using dots and dashes to indicate holes and slits for pierced design. Use small dots for fine lines and large dots for bold lines. Unless the design indicates otherwise, mark evenly spaced dots.

2 Cut metal to correct size, using tin snips, as on page 78, step 1 for the flat-surfaced door or for the recessed-panel door. Remove fingerprints and smudges from the metal by rubbing it with fine steel wool.

3 Tape the metal panel along all edges to the plywood, using wide duct tape. Center the pattern on the metal panel; tape in place. Cushion the work surface under the plywood with several layers of newspaper.

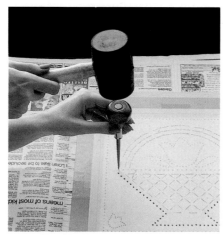

4 Hold piercing tool at right angle to metal surface, resting the point of tool on a dot in the pattern. Strike with mallet or hammer, driving point of tool through metal.

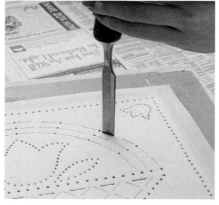

5 Complete entire design, using tool with larger point on larger dots and tool with smaller point on smaller dots. Use chisel or engraver for the dashes. Remove the pattern slowly, checking to be sure that all holes and dashes are pierced.

6 Remove fingerprints and smudges with fine steel wool. If you want to prevent metal from aging, apply aerosol acrylic sealer. Or allow metal to age naturally.

HOW TO APPLY A PIERCED METAL PANEL
TO A FLAT-SURFACED DOOR

MATERIALS

- Prefinished door.
- Flat decorative wood molding.
- Wood glue.
- Masking tape.
- Small brads.
- Miter box and backsaw.

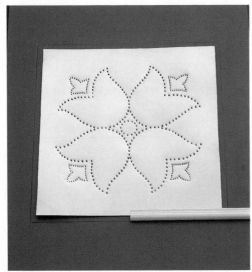

1 Mark the desired outer dimensions for molding frame on door, making sure corners are squared. Cut the metal panel with the length and width equal to these dimensions minus one width of molding in each direction. Pierce meal panel as on page 77, steps 1 to 6.

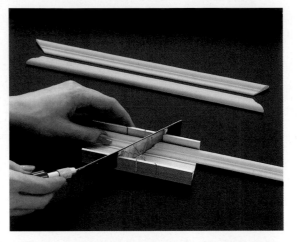

2 Measure and mark the length of upper and lower molding strips on outer edge; mark the angle of the cut. Cut the molding strips, using a miter box and backsaw. Check to see that the molding strips are exactly the same length. Repeat to cut side strips.

3 Paint or stain the moldings. Mark the placement of nail holes slightly toward the outer edge of the molding strips, 1½" (3.8 cm) from ends and at the center of each strip. Predrill nail holes, using drill bit slightly smaller than brads.

HOW TO APPLY A PIERCED METAL PANEL
TO A RECESSED-PANEL DOOR

MATERIALS

- Prefinished door.
- ¼" (6 mm) quarter-round wood molding or flat decorative molding.
- Miter box and backsaw.
- Wood glue.
- Small brads.

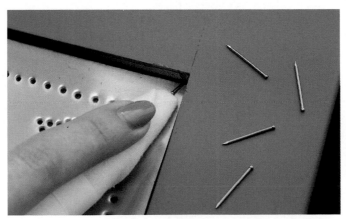

1 Cut the metal panel to exact measurements of recessed panel. Pierce metal as on page 77, steps 1 to 6. Secure the metal inside the recess with small brads inserted at an angle; to prevent scratching the metal, push brads in place using a screwdriver covered with cloth.

2 Cut quarter-round or decorative molding to fit inside the edge of the recess, using miter box to miter corners.

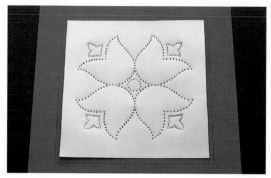

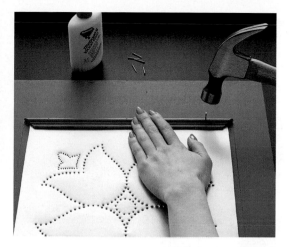

4 Center pierced metal panel on door along marked lines for frame. If door is not lying horizontally, secure metal panel temporarily with masking tape.

5 Apply wood glue sparingly to the back of the upper molding strip, toward the outer edge, using finger. Position molding strip on the door, aligning it with the markings and overlapping upper edge of the metal panel; secure with brads, leaving brads slightly raised.

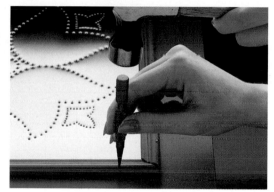

6 Attach molding strips for sides of panel, applying glue to the back and placing brads at the upper corners only. Attach lower strip, making sure frame is square. Secure the remaining brads for the sides of frame.

7 Countersink brads, using nail set. Touch up nail holes and mitered corners with paint, or fill them with putty to match stain.

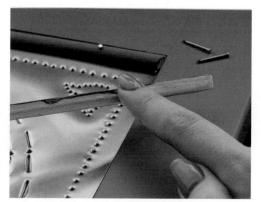

3 Paint or stain the moldings. Mark the placement of nail holes slightly toward outer edge of molding strips, 1½" (3.8 cm) from ends and at center of each strip. Predrill nail holes, using drill bit slightly smaller than brads.

4 Apply wood glue sparingly to the back of molding strips, toward the outer edge, using finger. Position molding strips on door, around inner edge of recessed area; nail in place, leaving brads slightly raised.

5 Countersink brads, using a nail set. Touch up nail holes and mitered corners with paint, or fill them with putty to match the stain.

PRESSING FLOWERS

Pressed flowers make beautiful accents for many home decorating accessories, including floral sun catchers and botanical artwork (pages 84 to 89). The pressed flowers are inexpensive to make, using flowers from your garden and a handmade flower press.

THE FLOWER PRESS

Although you have probably pressed flowers between the pages of a heavy book, a flower press will produce better results. The flower press consists of wooden front and back covers, with layers of corrugated cardboard between them. The flowers are pressed between the cardboard layers, with blotter paper or blank newsprint on both side of the flowers. The blotter paper or newsprint absorbs the moisture from the flowers. The wing nuts on the corners of the press are tightened, to flatten the flowers as they dry.

FLOWER SELECTION

Flowers dried in a flower press usually retain much of their original color and take on a translucent quality. Select flowers that are in perfect condition, dry, and free of insects. Almost any flower can be preserved in a press, but some work better than others. Flat flowers and flowers with only a few petals, such as pansies

and violas, can be pressed intact and, when pressed, will retain their natural form. However, to press flowers with thick, hard centers, you must take the flowers apart, petal by petal, because of the difference in thickness between the flower parts. Then reassemble the flowers, gluing the petals together, when you use them in a project. The thick, hard centers must be pressed in a different layer of the flower press from the petals. Or discard the centers and substitute similar, but flatter, centers from another variety when reassembling the flowers.

Bell-shaped flowers, which are difficult to take apart, generally look better as three-dimensional, rather than pressed, flowers. Rose petals press well, but they cannot be reassembled into the original shape of the rose. Rosebuds can be sliced in half with a razor blade, and then pressed.

PRESSING THE FLOWERS

The flowers must remain in the press until they have lost all their moisture and feel papery. This usually takes one to two weeks, depending on the thickness of the flowers and the amount of moisture in the flowers at the time they were put into the flower press. Changing the sheets of blotter paper or the newsprint after several days speeds the process and prevents the flowers from

mildewing and browning; however, you risk damaging the flower when it is transferred to the fresh paper. To remove the flowers from the press, either when changing the paper or when flowers are completely dry, use tweezers with flat, rounded ends, such as those designed for stamp collecting. The sheets of blotter paper or newsprint can be reused after they have dried, provided they are not stained with mildew or dyes from the flowers.

Keep a log, listing the types of flowers that are being pressed in each layer, the dates they were put into the press, and the dates the blotter paper was changed. You may also want to include other information, such as where the flowers were gathered. By keeping a record, you will know exactly what is in the press without disturbing the materials before they are dry.

MATERIALS

- Two pieces of ½" (1.3 cm) plywood or medium-density fiberboard (MDF), each 9¾" × 12¼" (25 × 31.2 cm).

- Four ¼" × 3½" (6 mm × 9 cm) bolts with wing nuts and washers.

- Several sheets of corrugated cardboard with smooth, flat surfaces on both sides, each 9½" × 12" (24.3 × 30.5 cm).

- Several sheets of 19" × 24" (48.5 × 61 cm) blotter paper, each cut into four pieces that measure 9½" × 12" (24.3 × 30.5 cm); blank newsprint may be substituted, but do not use paper toweling or other textured papers that could imprint the flowers.

- Adhesive tabs, for numbering the cardboard layers.

- Mat knife; 220-grit sandpaper; drill and ¼" drill bit.

- Tweezers with flat, rounded ends, such as tweezers used by stamp collectors, for removing pressed flowers.

- Small notebook, for recording data.

- Plastic sleeves, wax paper, or wax paper envelopes used by stamp collectors, for storing the pressed flowers.

HOW TO MAKE A FLOWER PRESS

1 Measure ¾" (2 cm) from edges at each corner of wooden top cover; mark. Drill holes in the cover, using ¼" drill bit.

2 Use top cover as guide for marking position of holes in bottom cover. Drill holes in bottom cover. Sand all edges and surfaces of the covers.

3 Stain or paint covers, if desired. Decorate the top cover, if desired, gluing dried floral materials or other embellishments in place.

4 Measure and mark the sides of the cardboard 2" (5 cm) from each corner. Using straightedge, draw a diagonal line across each corner, connecting the marks. Trim off each corner, using a mat knife.

5 Repeat step 4 for all pieces of cardboard and for the sheets of blotter paper or newsprint. Attach adhesive tabs to the edges of the cardboard pieces, labeling each of the layers consecutively.

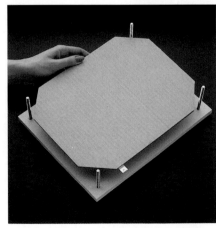

6 Assemble the press by putting the bolts through the back cover, from outside to inside. Lay the back cover on a flat surface, with inside facing up. Center the first sheet of cardboard over the cover.

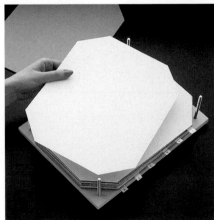

7 Stack two sheets of blotter paper or four sheets of newsprint on top of the cardboard. Repeat the layers of cardboard and paper, ending with a piece of cardboard.

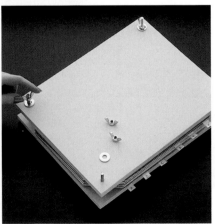

8 Insert the bolts through top cover. Place washers over the bolts, and secure with wing nuts.

HOW TO PRESS FLOWERS

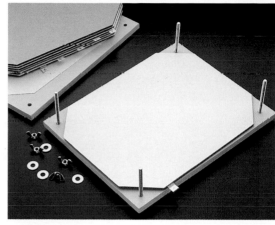

1 Remove top cover of the press, and remove all layers except the first piece of cardboard and one sheet of blotter paper or two sheets of newsprint.

2 Cut the stems close to flowers. Arrange the floral materials to be pressed on blotter paper or newsprint, allowing 1" (2.5 cm) of space around each item. Press materials of the same thickness on each layer.

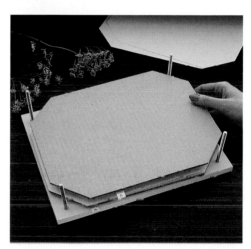

3 Cover with one sheet of blotter paper or two sheets of newsprint; then cover with one piece of cardboard.

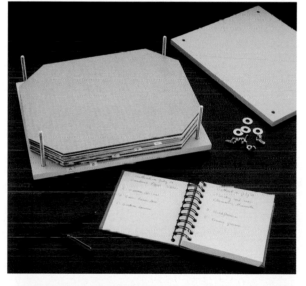

4 Repeat steps 2 and 3 for any additional layers, sandwiching floral materials between the blotter paper or newsprint and separating each of the layers with cardboard. Keep a record of the items being pressed on each layer, along with the date they were put into the press and where they were gathered.

5 Insert bolts into corners of top cover; place a washer and a wing nut over the bolt at each corner. Secure the cover, tightening wing nuts as far as possible. Retighten wing nuts every day until they are fully tightened.

6 Check floral materials after one to two weeks to see if they are completely dry; take care not to disturb other layers. When dry, remove floral materials carefully, using tweezers, and store them flat in plastic sleeves, between layers of wax paper, or in wax paper envelopes. Label contents. Store the pressed flowers away from light and humidity.

PRESSED-FLOWER SUN CATCHERS

Sun catchers reflect sunlight from a window, casting prismatic light on surfaces in the room. The paper-thin pressed flowers in these sun catchers are translucent and brilliant in color.

Make the pressed flowers as on pages 80 to 83, using flowers from your garden. Then encase the flowers between a layer of precut beveled glass and a layer of extra-thin glass cut to size using a glass cutter. The outer edges of the sun catcher are sealed with copper foil tape.

SPECIALTY SUPPLIES & TECHNIQUES

The supplies needed for sun catchers are available at any stained glass supply store. The precut glass bevels come in assorted sizes and shapes. Bevels with straight sides work best, because the foil tape does not wrap smoothly around the edge of a curve. Purchase a little more of the extra-thin glass than your project requires. It is quite inexpensive, and you will want to experiment with the cutting process. Also keep in mind that there may be some breakage. To keep breakage to a minimum, use light pressure when you score the glass, especially at the edges, and keep the wheel of the glass cutter lubricated with a light oil. Use safety glasses when you are cutting glass, to guard your eyes from flying glass chips. When cleaning up, use a hand broom, not your hand, to sweep the work surface.

- Beveled glass square, rectangle, or triangle in desired size.
- Pressed flowers, leaves, and grasses as desired.
- Extra-thin glass; glass cutter; grozing pliers.

- 24-gauge copper wire; ⅜" (1 cm) copper foil tape.
- Fine-tip marking pen; cork-backed straightedge; masking tape.

HOW TO CUT THE GLASS

1 Trace the shape of beveled glass piece onto extra-thin glass, using fine-tip marking pen. Use outer edges of the glass sheet as one or two sides whenever possible.

2 Place a straightedge along one marked line on the glass, from one edge of the glass sheet completely across to the opposite edge. Check to see that the wheel of the glass cutter (arrow) will line up exactly on the marked line.

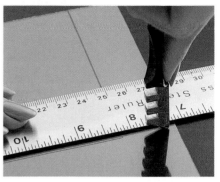

3 Hold the glass cutter perpendicular to the glass, with the wheel parallel to straightedge, beginning ⅛" (3 mm) from one edge of the glass. Hold the straightedge firmly in place with other hand.

4 Push or pull glass cutter, depending on which feels more comfortable for you, across the glass, from edge to edge, to score the glass; exert firm pressure, maintain a constant speed, and keep the glass cutter perpendicular to the glass. Ease up on the pressure as you score off the edges of the glass on the opposite side. Score the glass only once; do not repeat the process.

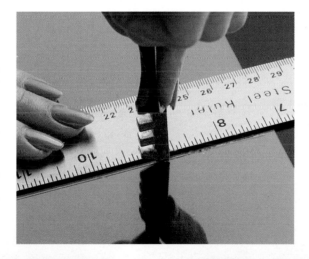

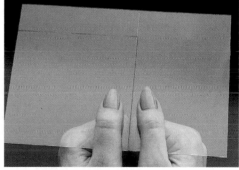

5 Hold the glass in both hands, with the scored line between your thumbs; curl your fingers under the glass, making fists, with knuckles touching each other.

6 Apply quick, even pressure as you roll your thumbs out from each other, turning your wrists upward; this breaks the glass along the scored line.

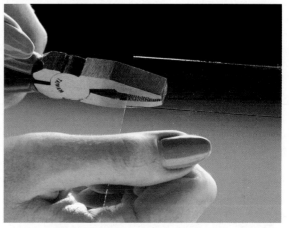

7 Repeat steps 2 to 6 for each of the remaining lines marked on the glass. For pieces that are too narrow to grasp with your fingers, use grozing pliers for safety and to obtain more leverage; hold the pliers at a right angle close to the end of the score and with flat jaw of the pliers on top of glass.

HOW TO MAKE A PRESSED-FLOWER SUN CATCHER
WITH A CORNER HANGER

1 Cut extra-thin glass (page 85) to the size of the beveled glass. Clean both surfaces of the beveled glass and the extra-thin glass piece with glass cleaner and lint-free cloth or paper towel.

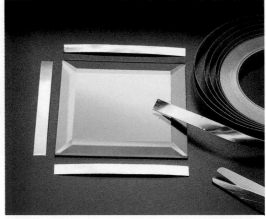

2 Cut a length of the foil tape to the exact measurement of each side of beveled glass.

3 Place extra-thin glass piece facedown on clean surface. Arrange pressed flowers and leaves on center of glass in an area not larger than the center portion of beveled glass; materials under the bevel would appear distorted.

4 Place beveled glass, flat side down, over the pressed flowers, aligning glass edges. Adjust flower placement, if necessary.

5 Apply small pieces of masking tape to all sides of the sun catcher to hold it firmly together, keeping the flowers in place.

6 Decide which corner will contain hanger. Make hanger by forming a loop in copper wire, and cut the wire ends so they extend at least halfway down each adjacent side.

7 Peel paper backing from the strip of foil tape for lower edge of sun catcher. Holding the layered pieces of glass firmly in one hand, apply the foil tape to lower edge, centering tape on outer edge of glass so equal amounts will wrap to front and back.

8 Fold the foil tape to the front and back, smoothing it in place.

9 Apply foil tape to any remaining sides of the sun catcher that will not contain the hanger wire.

10 Apply tape to the sides adjacent to upper corner of sun catcher, centering the hanger wire along the edges of the glass and encasing it under the strips of foil tape.

11 Smooth all sides of the foil tape firmly, using handle of wooden spoon or wooden craft stick to ease out any bubbles or gaps.

12 Suspend sun catcher in a window, using fine nylon thread. For greater impact, arrange several sun catchers in one window.

HOW TO MAKE A PRESSED-FLOWER SUN CATCHER WITH THE HANGER CENTERED ON ONE SIDE

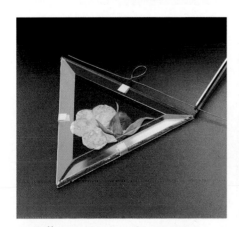

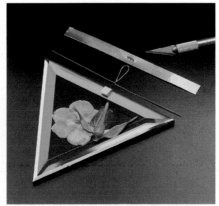

1 Follow steps 1 to 5, opposite. Decide which side will contain hanger. Make hanger by forming a loop in copper wire, and cut the wire ends so they extend to outer corners of the side.

2 Follow steps 7 to 9, opposite. Before removing paper backing from foil tape for upper side of sun catcher, cut small slit in center of foil tape, just large enough to insert the loop of the hanger.

3 Apply the tape to the upper side, centering wire along the edge of glass and encasing it under the tape. Complete sun catcher as in steps 11 and 12, above.

FRAMED BOTANICALS

Pressed flowers and leaves can be mounted in prematted frames for a classic wall arrangement. The natural beauty of pressed flowers surpasses that of botanical prints, at a fraction of the cost.

Single large leaves or clusters of small pressed flowers and grasses can be arranged on rice paper for a textural background. Then cover the botanical materials with a sheet of extra-thin glass to hold them securely, and place the layers in a purchased frame.

MATERIALS

- Inexpensive frame with a precut mat.
- Extra-thin glass.
- Glass cutter.
- Rice paper.

- Pressed flowers, leaves, or grasses (page 80).
- Double-stick framer's tape or craft glue.
- Brads; split-joint pliers.

HOW TO MAKE FRAMED BOTANICALS

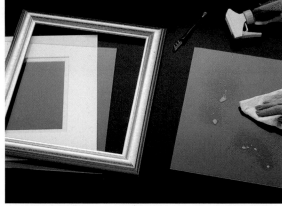

1 Remove the backing, precut mat, and glass from frame. Cut a piece of extra-thin glass, as on page 85, cutting it to same size as the glass provided with the frame. Clean both of the glass pieces thoroughly.

2 Cut rice paper to fit the backing provided with frame. Attach paper to backing at corners, using double-stick framer's tape or dots of glue.

3 Arrange pressed floral materials on the rice paper, checking to see that arrangement fits within mat opening.

4 Position extra-thin glass over pressed floral materials and rice paper. Position precut mat over extra-thin glass.

5 Position the original glass over precut mat and other layers; then position the frame over the glass.

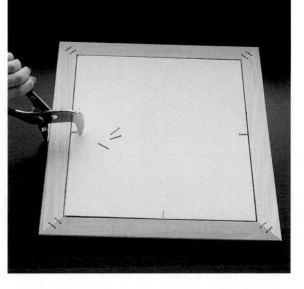

6 Turn frame over, keeping all layers firmly in place. Secure the layers into the frame, using small brads and split-joint pliers; pressure between layers keeps the flowers in place.

DECORATIVE BOXES

Decorative boxes grouped on a table can add interest to a room and cost very little. Small, sturdy, cardboard boxes you have on hand and inexpensive cardboard boxes purchased at a craft store can be wrapped with interesting papers for a novelty look.

For simplicity in covering the boxes, choose boxes that have attached, hinged lids. Or, if you have boxes with separate lids, convert them to hinged lids by attaching the lids as shown below.

Select inexpensive or recycled papers, such as old sheet music, maps, or newspapers. Create eye-catching collages for the lids from found items, such as trinkets, pieces of corrugated cardboard, torn papers, and old buttons.

MATERIALS

- Sturdy cardboard box with attached lid, or box with separate lid converted to attached lid; corrugated cardboard box is not suitable.
- Inexpensive or recycled paper, such as old sheet music, maps, or newspapers.
- Vinyl tape, 1" (2.5 cm) wide, for making a hinged lid.
- Thick craft glue.
- Sponge applicator.
- Miscellaneous found items, for lid embellishments.
- Ribbon or small tassel, for optional lid tab.
- Ruler; mat knife; scissors.

HOW TO MAKE A HINGED LID ON A BOX

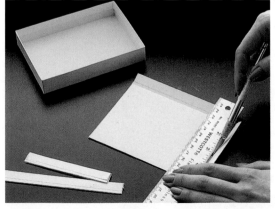

1 Remove the sides from the lid of the box, using mat knife.

2 Place lid piece on top of box, with back edges even. Secure it with vinyl tape along the back edge, keeping lid in closed position.

HOW TO MAKE A DECORATIVE BOX

1 Measure the box accurately from one back edge, around the sides and front, to the opposite back edge. Draw a rectangle on back side of paper to be used for covering the box, with length of rectangle equal to this measurement; width of rectangle is equal to height of box. If paper is not large enough, sheets may be pieced together by overlapping the edges and gluing them together.

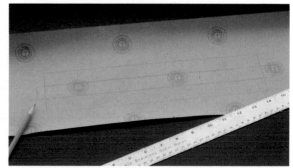

2 Draw ½" (1.3 cm) extensions on each side. Draw 1" (2.5 cm) extension on upper edge, excluding the side extensions. Draw 1" (2.5 cm) extension for lower edge, including side extensions. Cut paper on marked lines.

HOW TO MAKE A DECORATIVE BOX

3 Apply craft glue to the back side of paper, using sponge applicator; dilute glue with water, if necessary, just enough to spread easily.

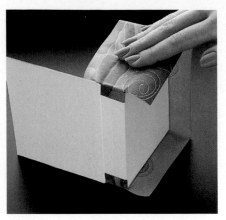

4 Affix paper to front and sides of the box, wrapping the ½" (1.3 cm) extensions around to the back of box and allowing 1" (2.5 cm) to extend at top and bottom.

5 Clip upper edge of paper at each front corner. Smooth extension to inside of box on the front and sides, overlapping the paper at the corners as necessary.

6 Wrap extension onto the bottom of the box, mitering corners. Secure miters with glue.

7 Open the lid. Trace lid and back of box onto paper, marking the points where lid is attached.

8 Add ½" (1.3 cm) extensions to the front and sides of lid portion. Add ½" (1.3 cm) extension to lower back edge. Cut out paper.

9 Apply glue to back side of paper; affix it to lid and back of box, wrapping extensions to underside of lid and mitering the corners. Close lid. Wrap extension at lower back edge onto the bottom of the box.

10 Trace lid onto paper, for the lid lining. Add 1" (2.5 cm) extension on the back edge. Cut out paper, cutting ⅛" (3 mm) inside the marked lines on the front and side edges.

11 Glue a folded 3" (7.5 cm) length of ribbon or a small tassel to bottom of lid at center front, to form tab for lifting lid.

12 Apply glue to lid lining piece; affix it to bottom of lid. Smooth extension at back edge of lid to inside back of box.

13 Trace bottom of box onto paper. Cut out the paper, cutting ⅛" (3 mm) inside the marked lines. Apply glue; affix to outside of box bottom.

15 Embellish the lid with found items, arranging items as desired.

14 Close lid; secure with rubber bands or weight down the lid until glue is completely dry.

DECORATING WITH GREAT FINDS

*Using secondhand finds can add
personality and style to your home.*

If you like to decorate your home in a way that is
uniquely yours, you may have already discovered the
rare finds at antique stores, salvage yards and flea
markets. Among the growing number of people who
would rather seek out a garage sale or antique store
than shop at a mall, you may find yourself searching
through tables of castoffs until you uncover something
you feel compelled to own.

In your search, do not overlook the obvious places,
like your grandmother's attic. Perhaps you have old
windows and doors stored in the garage, or you may
even have some weathered architectural pieces leaning
against an old building or storage shed.

The ultimate reward in the discovery of great finds is
in creating a home with a style of your own. Display a
collection of antique purses, hang a vintage quilt,
or simply prop an old, weathered door against the
wall. You will find that items worn with age add a
special character to your home.

The "treasures" you find might need to be cleaned up
a bit or refurbished. But, as you can see by paging
through this chapter, the end result can be impressive.

GOLD-LEAF FINISH
WITH AN AGED LOOK

Agold-leaf finish with an aged look gives found objects with intricate carved or raised detailing a rich, Old World effect. With its timeless, mellow look, this finish is often used for the picture frames of fine artwork found in museums. Because it may be used on wood, plaster, or cast-resin furnishings, it is also suitable for sconces, candlesticks, and small pieces of furniture. Although the finish requires several steps, the process is easy and the results are exquisite.

For this finish, use imitation gold leaf, sold in craft and art stores. For the dimensional effect, various materials are used in addition to the gold leaf, creating layers and depth. First, a base coat of paint is applied. Then the gold leaf is applied, followed by a clear acrylic sealer that protects the gold leaf from tarnishing. Because the gold leaf is almost translucent, the color of the base coat contributes to the color of the gold leaf. A red base coat, for example, gives a warm, rich gold finish while a white or gold base coat results in a lighter, brighter finish.

The remaining steps are designed to give the worn, Old World look to the finish. A heavy coat of latex or acrylic paint in taupe or cream is applied, then wiped away before it dries, except in the crevices and recessed areas. This is followed by a dusting of rottenstone powder, available at hardware stores, to add texture and aging to the gold-leaf finish.

MATERIALS

- Imitation gold leaf; water-based gold-leaf adhesive.
- Latex or acrylic paint in red or gold, for the base coat.
- Latex or acrylic paint in taupe, beige, or cream, for the top coat.
- Polyvinyl acrylic primer, if item is plaster.
- Rottenstone powder.
- Aerosol clear acrylic sealer.
- Paintbrushes, for applying paint, gold-leaf adhesive, and rottenstone powder; clean, lint-free rags; terry-cloth towel.

Gold-leaf finish
may vary, depending
on the paint colors
used in the process,
as you can see in
these close-up details.
The sconce (near
right) has a red base
coat under the gold
leaf, with a beige
top coat. The frame
(far right) has a
base coat of gold
paint under the gold
leaf, with a cream
top coat.

HOW TO APPLY A GOLD-LEAF FINISH WITH AN AGED LOOK

1 Clean the found object as necessary. Apply a base coat of red or gold paint; allow to dry. If the item is plaster, apply a polyvinyl acrylic primer before applying the base coat.

2 Apply an even, light coat of gold-leaf adhesive, using paintbrush. Allow to set until clear, about one hour; surface will be tacky, but not wet.

3 Cut sheet of imitation gold leaf into smaller, manageable pieces, using scissors. Hold the gold leaf between the supplied tissues; avoid touching it directly with your hands. Slide the bottom tissue from underneath the gold leaf. Touching the top tissue, press gold leaf in place over the adhesive.

4 Remove top tissue. Using soft, dry paintbrush in an up-and-down motion, gently tamp the gold leaf in place to affix it. Then smooth gold leaf, using brush strokes.

5 Continue to apply additional pieces of the gold leaf, overlapping them slightly; the excess gold leaf at the edges will brush away.

6 Fill in any gaps between sheets of gold leaf as desired by applying adhesive and scraps of gold leaf. Apply two coats of aerosol clear acrylic sealer; allow to dry.

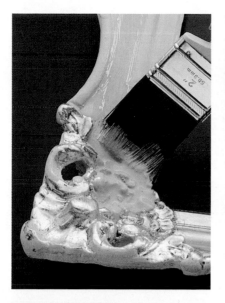

7 Apply a heavy coat of latex or acrylic paint in a burnt umber, taupe, beige, or cream, over the gold leafing. On large project, work on one section at a time, applying the paint and completing step 8 before moving on to the next section.

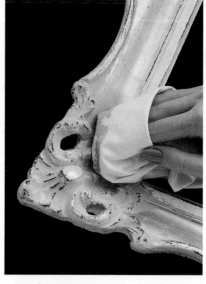

8 Allow paint to partially dry; when paint begins to set, wipe paint off with a clean, lint-free rag. Start by applying light pressure, and then rubbing harder, if necessary. Remove most of the paint in the smooth areas, leaving paint in the carved areas, the crevices, and corners. If paint is difficult to remove, a slightly damp rag may be used.

9 Sprinkle a generous amount of rottenstone powder over the entire project while paint is still slightly damp. Tamp the powder down, using a paintbrush.

10 Leave rottenstone powder on project for 20 minutes; then remove the excess powder with a soft-bristle paintbrush.

11 Buff the raised areas and edges very hard, using terry-cloth towel. Base coat should show in some areas, for a worn effect.

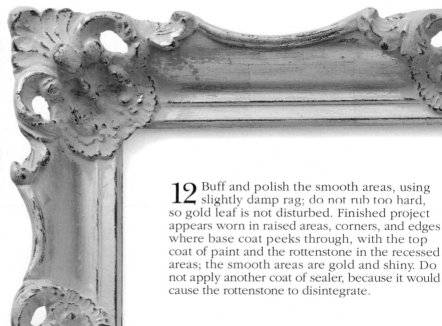

12 Buff and polish the smooth areas, using slightly damp rag; do not rub too hard, so gold leaf is not disturbed. Finished project appears worn in raised areas, corners, and edges where base coat peeks through, with the top coat of paint and the rottenstone in the recessed areas; the smooth areas are gold and shiny. Do not apply another coat of sealer, because it would cause the rottenstone to disintegrate.

LINING ARMOIRES

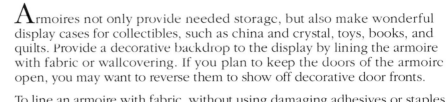

Armoires not only provide needed storage, but also make wonderful display cases for collectibles, such as china and crystal, toys, books, and quilts. Provide a decorative backdrop to the display by lining the armoire with fabric or wallcovering. If you plan to keep the doors of the armoire open, you may want to reverse them to show off decorative door fronts.

To line an armoire with fabric, without using damaging adhesives or staples, wrap heavy cardboard with the fabric and apply it to the inside of the armoire with pieces of self-adhesive hook and loop tape. A thin layer of polyester fleece, placed between the cardboard and the fabric, adds a light padding.

Before lining an armoire with wallcovering, lightly sand the wood in order to degloss the finish and ensure good adhesion. Most wallcoverings will adhere without applying a wallcovering primer. If a primer is used, returning the armoire to its original finish at some future date would be more difficult.

Armoires may be lined with wallcovering (opposite) or fabric (below) to neatly finish off the interior.

HOW TO LINE AN ARMOIRE WITH FABRIC

MATERIALS

- Mediumweight, firmly woven fabric.
- Polyester fleece.
- Self-adhesive hook and loop tape.
- Heavy cardboard, or foam-core board.
- Aerosol adhesive intended for use with fabric.
- Fabric glue.
- Mat knife.

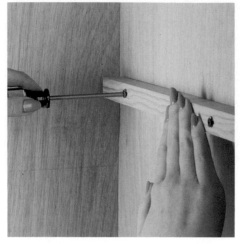

1 Remove any shelves and shelf supports from armoire.

2 Cut the cardboard ¼" (6 mm) smaller than the length and width of the armoire back, using a mat knife and straightedge. Check fit of cardboard in armoire.

3 Cut polyester fleece slightly larger than the cardboard. Apply aerosol adhesive to one side of cardboard; affix fleece to cardboard. Trim the edges of fleece even with edges of cardboard.

4 Cut fabric 4" (10 cm) larger than cardboard. Center the cardboard, fleece side down, on the wrong side of fabric. Wrap fabric around cardboard at the corners and sides as shown; glue in place.

5 Cut short strips of self-adhesive hook and loop tape. Press the hook side and loop side of tape together; affix to back of the armoire, at the corners and at intervals as desired.

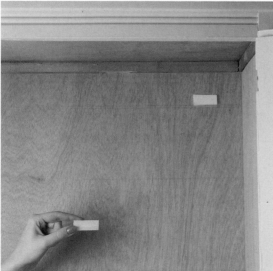

6 Position covered cardboard on armoire back; press into place, pressing against hook and loop tape strips, to affix cardboard to armoire. Repeat steps 2 to 5 for sides of armoire without shelves; position in armoire.

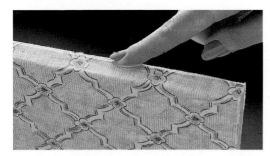

7 Cover the shelves, if any, using rectangle of fabric cut to fit length of shelf; wrap the fabric around shelf, securing overlapped fabric on the back edge. Secure raw edges of fabric, using glue diluted with water.

8 Reinstall the shelf supports and the shelves. Cover sides of the armoire with shelves by cutting cardboard ¼" (6 mm) smaller than the length and width of each section between shelves. Cover the cardboard and install as in steps 3 to 6. This method may also be used to cover the bottom of armoire and any framed insets.

HOW TO LINE AN ARMOIRE WITH WALLCOVERING

MATERIALS

- Wallcovering; wallcovering adhesive, if necessary.
- Aerosol clear acrylic sealer; sandpaper; tack cloth.
- Smoothing brush; seam roller or brayer.
- Razor knife; straightedge.

1 Remove shelves and shelf supports. Apply aerosol clear acrylic sealer to interior; sand lightly to degloss the surface. Wipe with tack cloth. Cut wallcovering strip 1" (2.5 cm) wider and longer than side of the armoire. Moisten the prepasted wallcovering, or apply wallcovering adhesive. Position the wallcovering, and then smooth in place; extend onto back and bottom for ½" (1.3 cm), clipping as necessary.

2 Trim the wallcovering at the upper and front edges, using a straightedge and a razor knife.

3 Cut the wallcovering strip or strips 1" (2.5 cm) longer than back of armoire; apply the first strip to back, lapping over extension at side of armoire. Trim upper edge.

4 Apply additional strip or strips to the back of armoire, trimming last strip to extend ½" (1.3 cm) onto the side. Cut and apply wallcovering to the remaining side, lapping over back extension and trimming upper and front edges.

5 Cut wallcovering to fit bottom; apply. Cover the shelves with wallcovering as in step 7, above, applying the adhesive to entire piece. Locate the holes for shelf support hardware; reinstall shelf supports and shelves.

For a creative accessory, turn an old window into a wall mirror, providing an element of surprise in your home decorating.

To make a mirror from an old window, simply remove the glass, replacing it with mirrors that are cut to fit within the window openings. On most window frames, the glass is secured with glazing and glazing points that need to be removed. The easiest way to remove the glazing is by softening it with a heat gun and scraping it off with a putty knife. An inexpensive heat gun will work well for this purpose; heat guns may also be rented. The mirror can then be held in place with glazing points only.

Cabinet doors with windows are usually assembled with a narrow wood beading that holds the glass in place. The beading can easily be removed by prying it off; it can then be replaced after the mirror is inserted.

Old windows are easy to find at salvage yards, antique stores,

Old windows *are converted into wall mirrors by replacing the glass with custom-cut pieces of mirror. The window shown above has a stained finish; a single mirror pane is secured using the window's wood beading. Opposite, a weathered window has several small panes, held in place with glazing points.*

and thrift stores, at affordable prices. Select one that has a sturdy frame, to ensure that it will support the mirror securely.

Window frames with mullions are especially attractive when used for mirrors. On some windows, each mullion frames a separate pane of glass; for these windows, a separate mirror must be cut to fit within each opening. Other window frames with mullions have a single opening with one large sheet of glass set into it, and the mullions are simply used as a decorative trim placed in front of the glass.

Mirrors may be ordered in custom sizes at glass supply stores and specialty mirror stores. Remove the old glazing and glass before ordering the mirrors, so you can accurately measure the openings of the window frame. Measure each opening individually to check for any variance in the sizes. Record the measurements for each opening on a sketch of the window.

MATERIALS

- Old window.
- Mirror of ⅛" (3 mm) thickness, cut to fit within rabbet, or recess, of each opening.
- Mat board, for backing.
- Glazing points, if old window has glazing.

- Two swivel hangers and screws, to mount onto back of mirror frame; two picture hangers or mirror hangers, to mount onto wall. Select hangers that will support the weight of the mirror.
- Heat gun; putty knife.

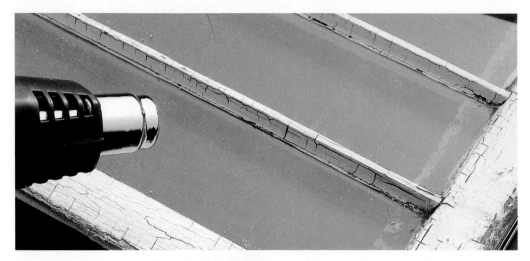

1 **Window with glazing and glazing points.** Soften the glazing around the edges of glass panes, using a heat gun on a high setting; hold the heat gun 4" (10 cm) from glazing, until the surface is heated. Stop heating if the paint begins to bubble.

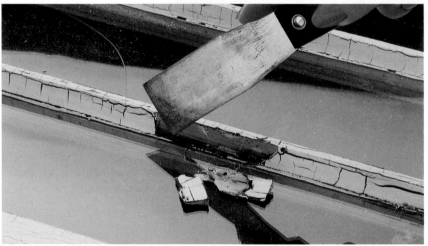

2 Scrape glazing with a putty knife to remove it. If necessary, repeat the process of softening and scraping the glazing. Take care to remove the glazing from corners of opening.

3 Pry out the metal glazing points that are set into the wood next to the glass, using screwdriver. Allow glass to cool.

4 Remove glass panes. Scrape off any remaining glazing from wood moldings. Clean the window frame and preserve the finish. Or apply a finish with an aged look, if desired.

5 Insert the mirrors, facedown, into the openings. Cut mat board to same sizes as openings; place on top of mirrors. Mat boards prevent the silver on back of mirror from becoming scratched.

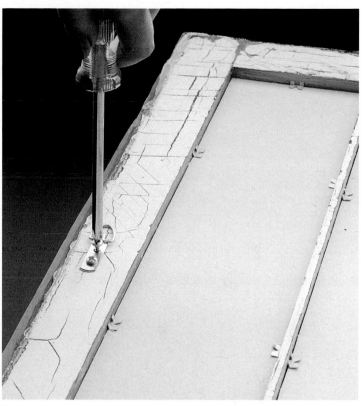

6 Insert glazing points into window frame on all sides of opening, pushing them into place with a putty knife.

7 Mark the placement for the swivel hangers on sides of frame, about one-third of the way down from the top; predrill the holes for the screws. Secure swivel hangers with screws.

8 Measure and mark placement for mirror or picture hangers on wall, equal to distance between swivel hangers on frame; use a carpenter's level to ensure that the marks are level. Secure mirror or picture hangers at markings. Hang mirror.

Window with wood beading. Pry off the wood beading, using screwdriver; remove the glass. Insert mirror and mat board as in step 5, opposite. Replace beading. Hang mirror as in steps 7 and 8.

POT RACKS FROM OLD WINDOWS

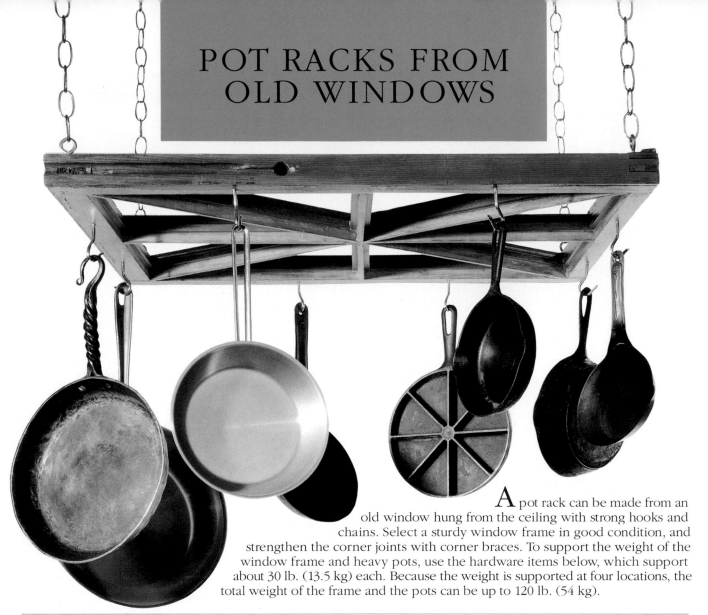

A pot rack can be made from an old window hung from the ceiling with strong hooks and chains. Select a sturdy window frame in good condition, and strengthen the corner joints with corner braces. To support the weight of the window frame and heavy pots, use the hardware items below, which support about 30 lb. (13.5 kg) each. Because the weight is supported at four locations, the total weight of the frame and the pots can be up to 120 lb. (54 kg).

MATERIALS

- Old window; corner braces.
- #6 zinc screw eyes and heavy chain, to hang frame.
- #6 zinc ceiling hooks, to hang pots.
- Swag hooks, to hang chains from ceiling.

HOW TO MAKE A POT RACK FROM AN OLD WINDOW

1 Remove the glazing and glass from the window frame (page 106). Clean the frame thoroughly, scraping off any loose paint; apply a fresh coat of paint or a clear acrylic finish.

2 Reinforce frame on top side with corner braces. Predrill holes and insert screw eyes near corners. Open one link of the chain, inserting screw eye; reclose link.

3 Predrill holes and insert ceiling hooks **(a)** on underside of frame. Secure swag hooks **(b)** into ceiling joists if possible, or use toggle bolts. Hang chains from swag hooks.

MORE IDEAS FOR OLD WINDOWS

Honeysuckle and silk ivy (above) encircle this crackled window frame, for a decorative wall display. To create the effect of a windowsill, a board is added at the bottom.

Scenic print (left) is displayed in the window of a cabinet door, rather than in a picture frame. The print was mounted as for a mirror (pages 105 to 107).

SHELVES FROM OLD SHUTTERS

Shutters contribute a casual feeling to a room, while offering interesting texture and color. Old shutters are easily adapted for a variety of new uses, including the decorative corner shelving units shown here and the creative display ideas on pages 112 and 113.

For a wide selection of old shutters, visit a salvage yard that has building materials. If you find painted shutters that have not yet weathered, you may want to apply a finish, for an aged look. If you prefer a stained wood finish in good condition, you may find more suitable shutters at antique stores, but you can expect to pay more for them.

To make corner shelves from shutters, select shutters, select shutters that are structurally solid and unwarped. Cut the triangular shelves from lumber, and trim the diagonal edges of the shelves with wood moldings.

MATERIALS

- Two shutters of the same size.
- Medium-density fiberboard or plywood in desired thickness, for shelves.
- Shelf molding or panel molding, for edges of shelves.
- ½" × ½" (1.3 × 1.3 cm) cove or inside corner molding, for shelf supports.
- ½" × ¾" (1.3 × 2 cm) parting stop, cut 2" (5 cm) shorter than shutters, to join shutters.
- 17 × 1" (2.5 cm) brads, for attaching moldings.
- Finish nails, for attaching parting stop and shelf supports.
- Wood glue; jigsaw; drill; ¹⁄₁₆" drill bit.

Corner shelves *made from old shutters may stand on the floor (left) or hang on the wall (below). To hang the shelving unit, use three sawtooth hangers, one near the corner and two at the outer edges of the shutter frame. Rubber bumpers, placed at the bottom, keep hanging shelves level.*

HOW TO MAKE SHELVES FROM OLD SHUTTERS

1 Cut one end of panel molding **(a)** or shelf molding **(b)** for shelves at 45° angle, using miter box, with direction of angle as shown. Measure angled edge as indicated; do not measure the rabbet, if using panel molding.

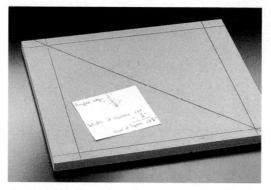

2 Add ⅛" (3 mm) to the measurement from step 1; subtract from width of the shutter. Mark a square this size on lumber for shelves; draw a diagonal line through square. Using a jigsaw, cut lumber on marked lines to make two shelves. Cut any additional shelves.

3 Align mitered end of molding to the diagonal edge of shelf; mark finished length and angle of miter cut at the opposite end. For each shelf, cut one molding strip, to be used as edge trim.

4 Cut one strip of cove molding for each shelf support, mitering the ends; length of the support is equal to length of the short side of triangular piece.

5 Apply wood glue to diagonal edge of the shelf; position the molding on edge. Predrill nail holes with ¹⁄₁₆" drill bit, at ends and center. Secure molding with brads. Set brads, using nail set.

6 Determine desired placement for shelves; mark the shutters with placement line for bottom of shelf. Mask off frame of shutters below marked line, using ⅜" (1 cm) strip of tape; mask off back edges of shutters.

7 Paint shutters, apply finish with aged look, or preserve finish; do not apply finish to areas that are masked off. Finish shelves, shelf supports, and parting stop to match shutters. Remove tape.

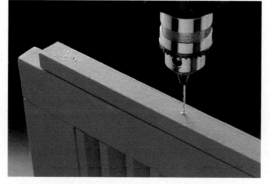

8 Position parting stop on shutter, centering it on length of shutter and aligning front edges. Predrill nail holes through parting stop and into frame, about 1" (2.5 cm) from ends and at 4" (10 cm) intervals. To secure parting stop, sand the edge, glue, and nail. Repeat to secure parting stop to remaining shutter, taking care to avoid previous nails.

9 Sand back edges of the shelf supports. Position supports with upper edge just covering the placement lines; predrill nail holes through support and into frame of shutter. Secure supports to shutters, using glue and nails. Place shelves on supports.

MORE IDEAS
FOR OLD SHUTTERS

Shutter, hung in the kitchen, serves as a rack for cooking utensils, lightweight pots, and copper molds. The items are hung from S-hooks.

Clean the shutter thoroughly, and apply a clear acrylic finish before using it to hang kitchen utensils. Secure the shutter to the wall, using drywall screws. If you are not able to screw into wall studs, use plastic anchors in predrilled holes to support the weight of the shutter.

Massive wall display features shutters instead of artwork. The shutters, given a weathered finish, are hung with swivel hangers as shown opposite.

Tabletop display (above) includes shutters that form a backdrop for a collection of accessories.

Shutters (right) are hung on the wall next to the window, for a country look. Hang the shutters as shown below.

Attach swivel hangers to the back of the shutter, about one-third down from the top; hang the shutter from picture hangers or mirror hangers.

CANDLESTICKS FROM OLD BALUSTERS

Balusters from staircases are often among the architectural finds in antique stores and salvage yards. These turned, and often quite ornamental, wooden posts are ripped out of old buildings before demolition. Available in various designs, they can easily become candlesticks, provided they are at least 2" (5 cm) in diameter. The balusters need not be in perfect condition. The usual nicks and scratches that come from years of wear add character to the piece. The newel post from the foot or landing of a demolished staircase may also be used for a candlestick.

To make a candlestick, cut a base and an upper platform from a separate piece of wood. If you are planning to maintain a natural or stained wood finish, select the type of wood used for the baluster, whenever possible, and stain the base to match. Or you may want to mimic the aged finishes of balusters.

HOW TO MAKE A CANDLESTICK FROM AN OLD BALUSTER

MATERIALS

- Old baluster, at least 2" (5 cm) in diameter.
- 1 × lumber, to be used for the base and upper platform of candlestick.
- Wood stain or paint in desired color or colors, optional.
- Wood glue.
- 5d nail, 1½" (3.8 cm) long, to hold candle in place.
- Backsaw; clamps; drill and ¹⁄₁₆" drill bit.

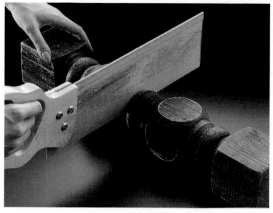

1 Clean the old baluster with mild soapy water; allow to dry. Saw post to desired height, using a backsaw.

2 Cut two square pieces from 1 × board for base of the candlestick, with one piece 1" (2.5 cm) and one 3" (7.5 cm) larger than diameter of post at bottom.

3 Cut two square pieces from the 1 × lumber for upper platform, with one piece ¾" (2 cm) larger and one 1½" (3.8 cm) larger than diameter of post at top.

4 Apply desired stain or paint finish to the post and squares of lumber.

5 Drill through center of larger piece for upper platform, using ¹⁄₁₆" drill bit. From bottom of piece, hammer nail into center hole; nail will protrude from top of piece, to be used for holding the candle in place.

6 Apply wood glue to the bottom of piece with nail; clamp to smaller piece for the upper platform. Apply wood glue to the bottom of smaller base piece; clamp to the larger base piece. Allow glue to dry.

7 Apply small amount of wood glue to bottom and top of post. Center base on bottom of post, with smaller section of base next to post. Center the upper platform on post, with smaller section of platform next to post. Clamp until glue dries.

TIERED PLATE TRAYS

Lovely tiered trays can easily be made from china plates, using lamp parts for the spacers between the plates and for the decorative top finial. To insert the lamp parts, a center hole is drilled through each plate, using a special drill bit. You may drill the holes yourself or have them drilled for you at a lighting repair or glass supply store.

To drill through ceramic or glass, use a ceramic drill bit; or use a hollow circular diamond drill bit and a drill press. To help prevent fracturing the plate while drilling, place mineral spirits or water in the plate to act as a lubricant and cooling agent, and drill slowly. Keep in mind that there is still some risk of fracturing the plate; for this reason, do not use valuable or irreplaceable pieces.

Glass, ceramic, or porcelain plates may be used. For a two-tier tray, choose a larger plate, such as a dinner plate or charger, for the bottom plate, and a smaller salad or dessert plate for the top one. For a three-tier tray, select three plate sizes so the tiers are graduated from larger to smaller, bottom to top.

To eliminate the need for a lamp base on the tiered tray, select a bottom plate that has a recess on the underside of at least 3/16" (4.5 mm), created by a rim. This allows the necessary space for the washers that secure the bottom plate. If the plate you select does not have an adequate recess on the underside, secure a lamp base under the plate to keep the tray from wobbling.

HOW TO MAKE A TIERED PLATE TRAY

MATERIALS

- Two or three plates in graduated sizes.
- ⅜" ceramic drill bit; or ⅜" hollow circular diamond drill bit and drill press.
- Lamp base, hex nut, and fender washer, if bottom plate does not have a recess of at least ³⁄₁₆" (4.5 mm) on underside.
- One threaded ¾" (2 cm) washer, if tray does not need a lamp base.
- Two ¾" (2 cm) rubber washers with ⁷⁄₁₆" (1.2 cm) center holes, for a two-tier tray; three rubber washers, for a three-tier tray.

- Two 1" (2.5 cm) brass washers with ⁷⁄₁₆" (1.2 cm) center holes, for a two-tier tray; three brass washers, for a three-tier tray.
- Three nipples, or threaded pipe, 1" (2.5 cm) long, to fit ⅛ IPS lamp pipe for a two-tier tray; five nipples, for a three-tier tray.
- One pair of decorative spacers with a combined length of 5" to 6" (12.5 to 15 cm), for a two-tier tray; or two pairs, for a three-tier tray.
- One decorative spacer for the top of the tray.
- One ⅛ IPS lamp finial or one ¼-27 lamp finial with reducer; one nipple, ⅝" (1.5 cm) long.

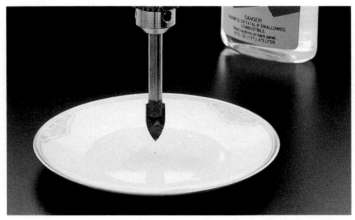

1 **Tiered tray without a lamp base.** Apply masking tape to each plate, centered on the front of the plate in an X; mark center. Pour mineral spirits into plate. Drill a ½" (1.3 cm) hole, using ceramic drill bit; drill slowly and keep the drill perpendicular to plate. Or drill hole with a hollow circular diamond drill bit and a drill press.

2 Screw a threaded washer to one end of a threaded nipple, so nipple does not extend beyond the threaded washer. Place rubber washer over other end of nipple.

3 Insert the threaded nipple into hole of bottom plate. Place 1" (2.5 cm) brass washer on the plate, over the nipple. Screw spacer onto nipple; do not overtighten, or the plate may crack.

4 Screw a threaded nipple into the top of first spacer; screw another spacer onto nipple.

5 Screw another nipple into top spacer; place a rubber washer on top of spacer, over nipple.

7 Screw on another spacer. Screw a nipple into spacer. Screw a reducer onto nipple, if ¼-27 lamp finial is used. Screw finial in place.

1 **Tiered tray with a lamp base.** Screw a hex nut onto one end of a threaded nipple. Place lock washer, then a fender washer over other end of nipple. Then insert nipple into hole of lamp base. Place a rubber washer on plate over nipple.

6 Repeat steps 3 to 5 if making a three-tier tray, using a medium-size plate. Place the top plate over nipple and rubber washer; place brass washer on plate, over nipple.

2 Complete tiered tray as in steps 3 to 7, opposite.

Shadow boxes (above and right) display cherished family memorabilia.

DISPLAYING
MEMORABILIA
IN SHADOW BOXES

Showcase cherished mementos of the past in shadow boxes. These frames have deep sides that allow you to mount dimensional items, such as jewelry, watches, and other memorabilia. Shadow boxes are available in many styles and finishes and can be ordered in the desired size and depth at framing shops.

Foam-core board, wrapped with fabric, is used for the mounting board and to line the sides of the frame. For conservation framing, use acid-free foam-core board and natural-fiber fabric, such as 100 percent silk, linen, or cotton.

To determine the shadow box size you need, arrange all the objects to be framed on a sheet of craft paper, making sure to allow the desired amount of space around each item. Mark the frame size, and outline the items on the paper to record the placement. To determine the frame depth, measure the deepest item; add ½" (1.3 cm) to this

measurement to allow for the frame assembly. Order the shadow box and the glass to these measurements.

Several methods may be used for mounting items. Photographs and documents can be hinge-mounted, using linen framer's tape. Textile items, such as baptismal gowns and handkerchiefs, can be secured to the mounting board with small hand stitches. Many other items, such as earrings, lockets, and fishing poles, may also be secured with hand stitches. For inconspicuous stitches, use a thread that matches the item. Monofilament fishing line also works well for any items and is strong.

Lightweight items that cannot be stitched in place, such as plates, may be secured with clear silicone glue, available at hardware stores. This glue stays flexible and can be removed without damaging the item. Plastic clips designed for mounting items are available at framing stores in several sizes and styles to hold a variety of objects, including plates, pipes, coins, spoons, and fishing poles.

HOW TO MAKE A SHADOW BOX DISPLAY

MATERIALS

- Wooden shadow box.
- Natural-fiber fabric, such as 100 percent silk, linen, or cotton.
- ¼" (6 mm) acid-free foam-core board.
- Double-stick framer's tape, or ATG tape.
- Gummed linen framer's tape.
- Clear acrylic finish; paintbrush.
- Utility knife; cork-backed metal straightedge.
- Needle; thimble; thread; fishing line; clear silicone glue; or plastic mounting clips, such as Mighty Mounts™, as needed for mounting various items.

1 Seal unfinished wood of shadow box, using clear acrylic finish; allow to dry. Place glass in shadow box.

2 Mark strip of foam-core board ⅛" (3 mm) shorter and ⅜" (1 cm) shallower than inside top dimensions of the shadow box. Score repeatedly on marked lines, using utility knife and straightedge, until board is cut through. Repeat to cut strip for inside bottom.

3 Cut fabric 2" (5 cm) larger than each strip of foam-core board. Secure double-stick framer's tape to the foam-core board along all the outer edges. Center foam-core board, tape side up, on wrong side of fabric. Wrap fabric firmly around the long sides; press in place onto tape.

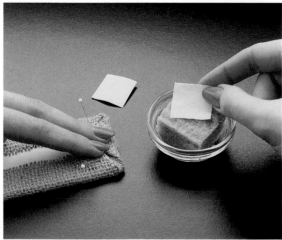

4 Wrap the fabric around ends, folding mitered corners; secure to tape. Secure the folded fabric at the corners, using moistened strips of linen framer's tape.

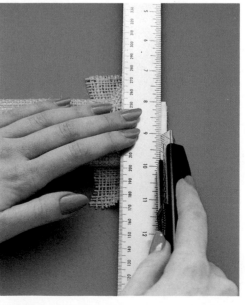

5 Position top and bottom pieces in frame; pieces should fit snugly without buckling. Repeat steps 2 to 4 for the side pieces. Check the fit of all pieces. If necessary, adjust size of pieces by peeling back fabric, then trimming the foam-core board and rewrapping it.

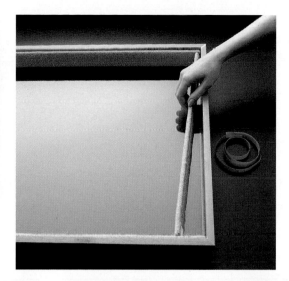

6 Cut mounting board ¼" (6 mm) smaller than the frame opening dimensions. Wrap mounting board with fabric as for side pieces. Check fit of mounting board; adjust, if necessary.

7 Remove the glass and clean it on both sides thoroughly, using a glass cleaner and a lint-free cloth. Reposition glass in frame. Cut strips of double-stick framer's tape; secure to back of each piece for sides of frame. Secure top and bottom pieces to frame, then side pieces.

8 Attach the items to the mounting board (below); attach photographs, if desired, as for mounting without a mat.

9 Place mounting board in frame. Recheck the display and glass for lint or dust. Complete the frame assembly.

TIPS FOR MOUNTING ITEMS IN A SHADOW BOX

Hand stitches. Arrange the item on mounting board. Determine several locations where article can be supported with small stitches. Thread a needle with monofilament fishing line or thread that matches item. Using threaded needle and thimble, secure item, taking about three stitches through mounting board at each support location. From back of board, tie the thread tails, and secure them to board with linen framer's tape.

Clear silicone glue. Secure any lightweight items with a bead of clear silicone glue. Allow the glue to cure for 24 hours before placing backing board into frame.

Plastic clips. Mark the location for holder. Punch hole to the back side of mounting board, using an awl. Insert the holder, and press speed nut into place. Trim the post a scant ⅛" (3 mm) from nut, using utility scissors or pruning shears.

DECORATING
THE
OUTDOORS

*Enhance your natural surroundings
with outdoor accessories for the front
entrance, patio and garden.*

Accessories can beautify the front entrance of your
home, brighten a porch or patio, and add charm to the
garden and yard. Personalize your outdoor living space
with handcrafted items made from mortar and wood.

Add color with the abundant use of flowers in
container gardens and twig wreaths. Plant flowers in
planter boxes made to perfectly fit the railing of
your deck. Build your own customized trellises.

Make the garden and patio more fun and inviting,
using garden stones and tree tables. And welcome
wild birds to your yard with handmade birdhouses
and decorative feeders.

For added drama in the evenings, use string lights
to accent an arbor or a floodlight to highlight a
tree or unique garden statue. And line a walking
path with luminaries.

DECK RAIL PLANTERS

Add a colorful display of flowers along the railing of your deck, arranging them in custom planter boxes. The deck rail planter, designed to hold potted plants, is basically a four-sided bottomless box with spacers on the underside that hold it snugly in place over the rail. The pots and saucers rest directly on the deck rail. Made from cedar, the box may be constructed with the rough side of the boards facing out. Or, for a more refined finish on a painted box, use the smooth side of the boards facing out.

The planter can be custom-built to any length and has an outside width of 10" (25.5 cm). The inside width of the planter is 8½" (21.8 cm), and, when the planter box is placed over the rail, the inside height is 6¼" (15.7 cm); select plant containers that fit these inside dimensions. For planter boxes longer than 32" (81.5 cm),

add a center support, securing it to the front and back of the box. The center support prevents the box from warping.

Determine the desired length of the planter box; if you are planning to use specific sizes of pots and saucers in the box, keep in mind that the inside length of the box will be 2" (5 cm) shorter than the outside length. For a long box with a center support, the inside length is 2¾" (7 cm) shorter than the outside length. It may be helpful to draw a sketch, including the pots that will be used in the box.

When determining the lumber required, allow extra length, in order to avoid the placement of knots at the ends of cut pieces. This will prevent difficulty when cutting the pieces and when inserting the screws.

MATERIALS

- 1 × 8 cedar lumber.
- 8 × 3" (7.5 cm) galvanized drywall screws, or deck screws.
- 6 × 1⅝" (4 cm) galvanized drywall screws, or deck screws.
- Exterior wood glue, such as Titebond® II.
- Razor knife.
- Jigsaw or circular saw.
- Drill and ⅛" drill bit.

Deck rail planter *is a simple bottomless box. Spacer blocks on the underside straddle the railing for a snug fit. The flowerpots and saucers rest directly on the deck rail.*

HOW TO MAKE A DECK RAIL PLANTER

1 Mark desired length of planter on face side of 1 × 8 lumber, for front piece. Lightly score on marked line, using a razor knife; this prevents wood from splintering when cut. Cut front piece, using a jigsaw. Mark and cut back piece to same length as front piece.

2 Mark 8½" (21.8 cm) length on lumber, for end piece; score with razor knife, and cut with jigsaw. Repeat to cut remaining end piece and, if necessary, the center support piece.

3 Mark a line on end piece, parallel to grain of wood, 1" (2.5 cm) from the lower edge; score with razor knife and cut with jigsaw on marked line. Repeat for the remaining end piece and for center support. Set aside 1" (2.5 cm) strips, to use for spacer blocks in step 7.

4 Mark placement for three screws, ¾" (2 cm) from one end of front piece, with one mark 1" (2.5 cm) from upper edge, one 2" (5 cm) from lower edge, and one centered between the two marks. Repeat at opposite end of front piece. If box has center support, also mark placement for row of screws at center of board. Mark back piece the same as front piece.

5 Stand end piece upright. Position front piece against end piece, extending it ¼" (6 mm) beyond end piece. Predrill holes for screws, using ⅛" drill bit; secure with 3" (7.5 cm) screws. Repeat for remaining end piece.

6 Position center support, if used, at center of front piece. Predrill holes, and secure screws. Secure back piece to end pieces and center support.

7 Add ⅛" (3 mm) to width of deck rail; subtract this measurement from inside width of box. Cut spacer blocks from the 1" (2.5 cm) strips set aside in step 3, with length of each block equal to one-half this measurement. You will need two spacer blocks for each end piece and two for center support.

8 Glue spacer blocks to each side of end pieces and center support as shown, with the blocks offset ⅛" (3 mm) from the edges of front and end pieces; distance between the blocks is slightly wider than the deck rail. Predrill hole into each block, using ⅛" drill bit; secure blocks, using 1⅝" (4 cm) screws. Planter may be left unfinished or may be stained or painted as in step 9.

9 Apply exterior wood stain **(a),** or apply exterior primer, with two coats of primer on ends of boards. Then apply exterior paint **(b).**

TRELLISES

Trellises, with customized dimensions and detailing, are easy to make. Use trellises and climbing plants to add interest to a plain surface, such as a garage wall or fence. To create a nearly invisible plant support over a window, extend the trellis above the window, using monofilament fishing line.

More of a craft project than a woodworking project, trellises are made using parting stop, lath, and screen molding. Parting stop is used for the vertical legs of the trellis. Wider lath, sometimes called lattice, is used for the horizontal supports. A horizontal lath piece is secured to both the front and back of the trellis for all but the bottom horizontal support. Motifs, such as squares, diamonds, and arrows, are cut from screen molding and used to trim the trellis. Parting stop, lath, and screen molding are readily available at building supply stores.

When designing a trellis, take into consideration the space where it will be displayed and the anticipated height of the climbing plants that will be used with the trellis. For design interest, stagger the lengths of the vertical legs of the trellis. An odd number of legs is usually most attractive. Support tall trellises with three horizontal pieces of lath. Experiment, making sketches of possible designs until you find a pleasing arrangement. Trellis motifs can be customized to repeat a theme or design line found in surrounding pieces, such as furniture or fences.

For a subtle look, paint the trellis to match the surface it is placed against. Or paint the trellis in a contrasting color for a structure that makes a design statement year-round.

CLIMBING PLANTS

ANNUAL PLANTS		PERENNIAL PLANTS	
Asarina (Climbing Snapdragon)	Nasturtium	Clematis	Dutchman's Pipe
Morning Glory	Scarlet Runner Bean	Climbing Hydrangea	Porcelainberry
	Sweet Pea	Climbing Rose	Silver Lace Vine

MATERIALS

- ½" × ¾" (1.3 × 2 cm) pine parting stop, for vertical legs.
- ¼" × 1⅜" (6 mm × 3.5 cm) pine lath, for front and back horizontal supports.
- ¼" × ¾" (6 mm × 2 cm) pine or oak screen molding, for decorative embellishments.
- Drill and ¹⁄₁₆" drill bit.
- Exterior wood glue.
- #19 × ½" (1.3 cm) wire brads.
- Miter box and backsaw.
- Monofilament fishing line, 30-lb. (13.5 k) test, for combination wood and string trellis.
- Exterior primer; exterior paint.

Trellises can be designed for a variety of spaces. Opposite, a free-standing trellis is supported with metal stakes. Right, a trellis is customized to fit under and around a window.

HOW TO MAKE A WOOD TRELLIS

1 Draw sketch of trellis to the desired dimensions; allow for 4" to 8" (10 to 20.5 cm) between each vertical leg. Finished width of trellis is equal to sum of distance between vertical legs plus ¾" (2 cm) for each vertical leg. Plan for horizontal supports to be positioned at the bottom, about 2" (5 cm) from top, and about two-thirds the distance from the bottom. Additional supports may be added, if desired.

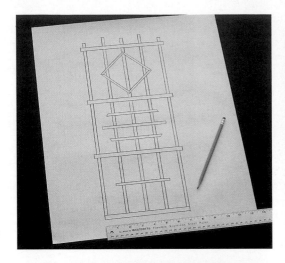

2 Mark and cut parting stop to desired length for each vertical leg; guide cuts, if desired, using miter box and 90° guide. For the horizontal supports on back side of trellis, cut pieces of lath with length equal to the finished width of trellis. Remaining horizontal supports for front of trellis are cut in step 5.

3 Place the vertical legs in desired arrangement, ¾" (2 cm) side up, on smooth, flat surface, with bottom of legs aligned. Place horizontal supports over legs as determined in step 1.

4 Glue and nail bottom horizontal support to legs, using two brads at each joint, and T-square or carpenter's square to ensure square corners; stagger placement of nails to help prevent splitting wood. Start at one side, and work toward the opposite side. Repeat to secure upper horizontal support, then middle supports.

5 Turn trellis over. Cut and position piece of lath over top and middle supports; lath can be cut to the width of trellis or with ends extending about 1" (2.5 cm) beyond legs. Secure each piece of lath with exterior wood glue and a brad at each vertical leg.

6 Cut pieces of screen molding as desired for embellishments, using tips on page 134. Position pieces, using glue. When the glue is tacky, secure with at least two brads; place scrap piece of lath under trellis for support when pounding brads.

7 Apply exterior primer to trellis; allow to dry. Paint as desired, using exterior paint. Mount trellis (page 134).

HOW TO MAKE A
COMBINATION WOOD & STRING TRELLIS

1 Determine the dimensions, and draw a sketch of the trellis, with the width at least 2" (5 cm) wider than width of window and upper edge of the top horizontal support just below lower edge of the window. Extend the outer legs to the desired height of the string portion of the trellis.

2 Cut the legs and the horizontal supports as in step 2, opposite. Arrange the trellis pieces as in step 3, opposite, position a horizontal support at bottom of the trellis and below the window. Mark the outer legs at upper edge of top horizontal support.

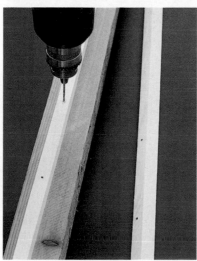

3 Mark holes for fishing line on ½" (1.3 cm) side of outer legs at 3" to 4" (7.5 to 10 cm) intervals, from marks to upper end. Drill at markings, using ¹⁄₁₆" drill bit.

4 Reposition outer legs, and assemble trellis as in steps 4 to 6, opposite. Mount trellis (page 134). Lace fishing line through drilled holes, starting at top of one leg and working from side to side as shown; cut the line, leaving excess at ends. Wrap fishing line around outer leg of trellis and tie in knot; pull line taut, and tie off remaining end.

TIPS FOR SCREEN MOLDING MOTIFS

Experiment with strips of paper cut ¾" (2 cm) wide to test the designs. Extend the ends of the design motifs beyond the legs of trellis when possible, to help prevent splitting the wood with brads.

Make paper patterns for diamonds, squares, and arrows, marking lines for miter cuts on both upper and lower pattern pieces. Cut patterns, and transfer markings to moldings.

Clamp sets of molding strips together to save time and ensure uniform lengths when making mitered cuts. Clamp pieces and make mitered cut at one end; repeat for mitered cut at opposite end.

HOW TO MOUNT A TRELLIS

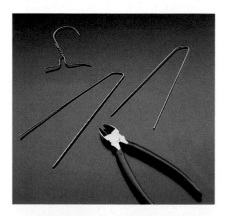

1 **Surface mount.** Cut clothes hanger, using wire cutter, to make two stakes as shown; discard the upper portion of hanger.

2 Position the trellis against a wall or a fence. Secure the bottom of trellis, using a coat-hanger stake at each end of the horizontal slat.

3 Secure the top of the trellis with a shoulder hook at each side; predrill the holes as necessary.

Freestanding mount. Insert metal stakes into the ground with distance between stakes equal to width of the trellis. Attach trellis to the stakes, using lengths of plastic-coated wire.

MORE IDEAS FOR TRELLISES

Discarded window guard (*above*) *provides a formal support for clematis.*

Rustic trellis (*left*) *is made using both straight and forked branches. Secure the branches with nails or wrapped wire. For branches that can be shaped, use freshly cut, green branches.*

Trellis motifs (*below*) *are painted to contrast with the trellis frame for a decorative effect.*

GARDEN STONES

Personalize your yard or garden with original stepping stones. Create stones to document special family events, such as birthdays or visits from family members. Make simple imprints in the garden stones, or decorate them with embedded gems or shells.

Made using mortar mix, garden stones are very inexpensive. Mortar mix is available at hardware stores and home center stores, and one bag will make many garden stones. Plastic plant liners and cardboard boxes are used as molds for making the stones.

Because the garden stones do not contain any gravel and are not reinforced, they are somewhat susceptible to breakage. To help prevent breaking, set the stone on a sand base, 1" to 2" (2.5 to 5 cm) in depth.

When making garden stones, work in a well-ventilated area and avoid inhaling dust from the mortar mix. You may want to wear a dust mask and eye protection. Wash thoroughly with water after handling the mortar mixture.

MATERIALS

- Mortar mix.
- Bucket, for mixing mortar.
- Wooden paddle, such as piece of pine lath.
- Metal spatula.
- Sturdy, flat cardboard box, such as a pizza take-out box, for mold of square garden stone.
- Round plastic plant liner, for mold of round garden stone.

HOW TO MAKE A GARDEN STONE

1 Round stone. Pour mortar mix into bucket; create a well in center of mix. Add water, and stir until mixture is the consistency of a thick paste; add more water as necessary, small amounts at a time. Mixture should be difficult to stir and not soupy.

2 Place round plastic plant liner on several layers of newspaper. Fill the mold with mortar mix. Using a wooden paddle, smooth the mortar level with the upper edge of the mold; repeat as necessary, adding mortar to any low areas.

3 Smooth surface of the mortar, if desired, using a metal spatula. Allow the mortar to cure for up to 5 minutes.

4 Embed items, such as marbles, beads, tiles, or shells, if desired.

Square stone. Cut lid from cardboard box, and insert it inside the box bottom. Apply packing tape to inside lower edges and inside corners, to seal them. Make garden stone, following steps 1 to 5, above.

5 Allow to dry 5 to 10 minutes. Draw designs, using the point of a pencil or a plastic knife, or make imprints as desired. Allow the mortar to cure for about 3 days. Remove stone from the mold.

BIRDHOUSES

Make a decorative birdhouse for the backyard, and enjoy the activity of nesting birds. This birdhouse is designed to be functional and can be finished for a variety of decorative looks.

The birdhouse is constructed with a floor about 4" (10 cm) square and a height of 8" (20.5 cm). This size is suitable for attracting many species of cavity-nesting birds, as listed in the chart opposite. The recommended diameter of the entrance hole and the height for mounting the birdhouse vary with the species of bird you are trying to attract.

To provide the necessary insulation, use lumber that measures 3/4" (2 cm) thick. To allow for cleaning, one side of the house pivots open. This also allows you to monitor the nesting or to remove nests if less desirable birds, such as sparrows, are occupying the birdhouse.

The house is easily made, using 1 × 6 lumber. The actual dimensions of these boards is 3/4" × 5½" (2 × 14 cm); however, the measurements may vary slightly. In order for the pieces of the house to fit together accurately, select a board that does measure 5½" (14 cm) in width. For a birdhouse that will withstand the elements for several years, use a long-lasting wood, such as cedar, redwood, or exterior-grade plywood. Pine can also be used; however, it is not as weather-resistant.

When embellishing birdhouses, take a few precautions. Do not apply any paint or preservative to the interior of the house, the inside of the entrance hole, or within 1/4" (6 mm) of the entrance hole on the exterior. Avoid painting the house with brightly colored paints, because this may deter birds from using it. If the birdhouse will be hung in direct sunlight, avoid dark colors, because the birdhouse may become too hot.

MATERIALS

- 46" (117 cm) length of 1 × 6 lumber such as cedar, redwood, pine, or exterior-grade plywood.
- 4d galvanized finish nails; drill and ¹⁄₁₆" drill bit.
- Spade bit, sized for desired size of entrance hole, according to chart below.
- Shoulder hook or other latch; screw eyes for hanging birdhouse.
- Handsaw, jigsaw, or circular saw.
- Exterior wood glue.
- 3" (7.5 cm) screws and drill bit, for vertical mounted birdhouse.

CUTTING DIRECTIONS

From 1 × 6 lumber, cut one 4" (10 cm) square for the bottom of house; if using ⁷⁄₈" (2.2 cm) cedar lumber, cut bottom of house 3¾" × 4" (9.5 × 10 cm). Cut one 5½" × 8¾" (14 × 22.4 cm) piece for the front of the house, two 4" × 5½" (10 × 14 cm) pieces for the sides of the house, and two 5½" × 6½" (14 × 16.3 cm) pieces for the roof of the house. For the back of a hanging birdhouse, cut one 5½" × 8¾" (14 × 22.4 cm) piece; or for the back of a tree-mounted or fence-mounted house, cut one 5½" × 11¾" (14 × 30 cm) piece.

BIRD	DIAMETER OF ENTRANCE HOLE	MOUNTING HEIGHT ABOVE GROUND
CAROLINA WREN	1½" (3.8 cm)	6 ft. to 10 ft. (1.85 to 3.07 m)
CHICKADEE	1⅛" (2.8 cm)	6 ft. to 15 ft. (1.85 to 4.6 m)
DOWNY WOODPECKER	1¼" (3.2 cm)	6 ft. to 20 ft. (1.85 to 6.18 m)
HOUSE WREN & WINTER WREN	1" to 1¼" (2.5 to 3.2 cm)	6 ft. to 10 ft. (1.85 to 3.07 m)
NUTHATCH	1¼" (3.2 cm)	12 ft. to 20 ft. (3.7 to 6.18 m)
TITMOUSE	1¼" (3.2 cm)	6 ft. to 15 ft. (1.85 to 4.6 m)

HOW TO MAKE A HANGING BIRDHOUSE

1 Trim the bottom piece diagonally across each corner, ½" (1.3 cm) from corner, to allow for drainage.

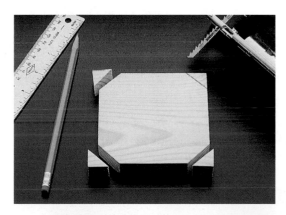

2 Mark center of upper edge on front piece. Position a carpenter's square at upper edge. Draw line from center mark to corresponding measurement at the side for pitch of the roof. Repeat for back piece. Cut on marked lines; if using jigsaw, make first cut from peak of roof down to side of house. Then cut opposite side, cutting from side of house toward peak.

3 Mark a line ¾" (2 cm) from the long edge of one roof piece. Cut on marked line so piece measures 4¾" × 6½" (12 × 16.3 cm).

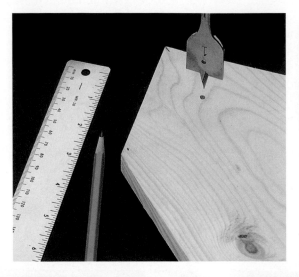

4 Mark a point on front piece, 6¾" (17 cm) from lower edge, centering the mark from side to side. Using spade bit, drill entrance hole, placing the tip of the blade on the marked point. Begin at low speed, gradually increasing speed as bit enters the wood.

5 Make several deep horizontal scratches below entrance hole on back side of front piece; scratches help young birds grip wood as they climb up to entrance hole.

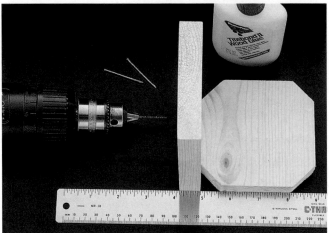

6 Apply wood glue to one side edge of bottom piece; if using ⅞" (2.2 cm) cedar, the 4" (10 cm) edges are the side edges. Align side piece to bottom piece so lower edges are flush. Predrill nail holes through side piece and into bottom, using 1/16" drill bit; secure with galvanized finish nails.

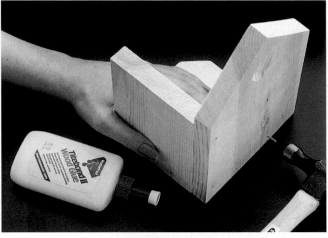

7 Apply wood glue to front edges of side and bottom pieces; align front piece with edges flush. Predrill holes, and secure front piece with nails. Repeat for the back piece.

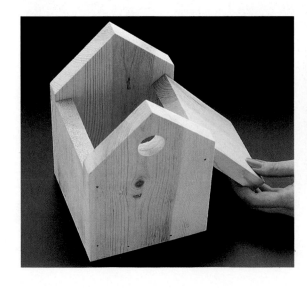

8 Align, but do not glue, the remaining side piece. Secure front and back pieces to the side piece, inserting one nail through front and one through back; position the nails about ⅝" (1.5 cm) from upper edge. This allows side piece to pivot as shown.

9 Apply glue to the upper edges of front piece and back piece on one side of house; position the shorter roof piece on house, with the back edges flush and with the upper edge of the roof aligned to peak of house.

10 Position the remaining roof piece in place; secure with glue. Predrill holes through both roof pieces; secure with nails.

11 Drill hole for shoulder hook or other latch in side of house front as shown; position the hole about 1" (2.5 cm) from the lower edge of board. Insert the shoulder hook to desired depth and pivot to secure the board or secure the latch.

12 Sand edges of birdhouse as necessary. Paint or stain as desired.

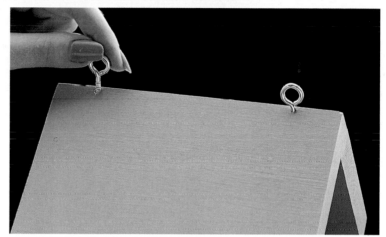

13 Attach screw eyes through roof near peak, for hanging birdhouse.

HOW TO MAKE A BIRDHOUSE THAT MOUNTS VERTICALLY

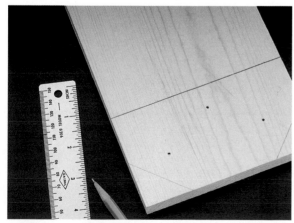

1 Mark a line 3" (7.5 cm) from one short edge of back piece; this is for aligning lower edge of bottom piece. Predrill three holes as shown for mounting birdhouse. Trim back piece diagonally across lower corners, if desired, about 1" (2.5 cm) from corners.

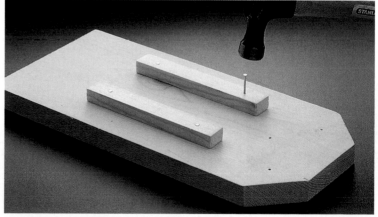

2 Nail two narrow wood strips to back of birdhouse as shown; this allows a space between the house and the surface it is mounted to, preventing any water from collection and soaking through the back piece. Continue as in steps 1 to 12, pages 139 to 141. Mount to fence post or tree, using screws inserted into drilled holes.

IDEAS FOR DECORATING BIRDHOUSES

Copper roof (right) develops a natural patina over the seasons. The copper sheets are wrapped around the wood roof pieces and nailed in place with copper weatherstrip nails. The birdhouse is painted in a blue-and-white checkerboard pattern.

Miniature doors and windows (left), sold as half-scale miniatures at dollhouse stores, embellish this house. The roof is shingled with dollhouse shakes.

Log-cabin style is created by nailing twigs to the exterior of this redwood birdhouse, and a chimney has been added. A large pinecone, painted green, is used as a pine tree.

Whimsical paint design *is used to personalize a pine birdhouse.*

Painted signs can add a splash of color and a touch of whimsy to the yard or garden. You can use the preassembled, unfinished wooden signs that are available in a variety of sizes and styles at craft stores. Purchased wooden cutouts, attached to wooden stakes, also make interesting signs. Or make your own custom signs, using a jigsaw and scraps of lumber.

Embellish the signs with lettering and simple painted designs, using items such as stencils, cookie cutters, or coloring books for inspiration. Small wooden cutouts can also be used as embellishments on larger signs.

Garden markers *(opposite) can be used to identify new plantings and add color to the garden.*

Party sign *(right) welcomes guests and directs them to a backyard party.*

TIPS FOR MAKING SIGNS

Use permanent opaque paint pens for lettering, or paint messages on the signs with a fine liner brush. If the signs are painted with acrylic craft paints, spray them with an aerosol clear acrylic sealer for more durability; signs painted with exterior paints do not require a sealer.

Apply wooden cutouts to signs, using exterior wood glue. For best adhesion, glue bare surfaces of wood together.

Make a stake for wooden cutouts by nailing a length of pine parting stop, a ½" (1.3 cm) square dowel, or purchased plant stakes to back of the sign; or secure stakes to the signs with exterior wood glue.

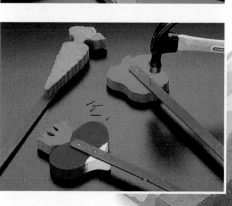

TREE TABLES

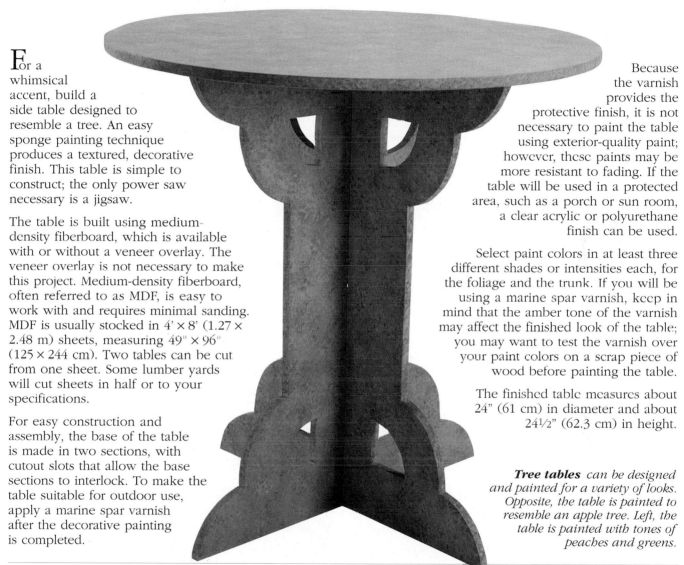

For a whimsical accent, build a side table designed to resemble a tree. An easy sponge painting technique produces a textured, decorative finish. This table is simple to construct; the only power saw necessary is a jigsaw.

The table is built using medium-density fiberboard, which is available with or without a veneer overlay. The veneer overlay is not necessary to make this project. Medium-density fiberboard, often referred to as MDF, is easy to work with and requires minimal sanding. MDF is usually stocked in 4' × 8' (1.27 × 2.48 m) sheets, measuring 49" × 96" (125 × 244 cm). Two tables can be cut from one sheet. Some lumber yards will cut sheets in half or to your specifications.

For easy construction and assembly, the base of the table is made in two sections, with cutout slots that allow the base sections to interlock. To make the table suitable for outdoor use, apply a marine spar varnish after the decorative painting is completed.

Because the varnish provides the protective finish, it is not necessary to paint the table using exterior-quality paint; however, these paints may be more resistant to fading. If the table will be used in a protected area, such as a porch or sun room, a clear acrylic or polyurethane finish can be used.

Select paint colors in at least three different shades or intensities each, for the foliage and the trunk. If you will be using a marine spar varnish, keep in mind that the amber tone of the varnish may affect the finished look of the table; you may want to test the varnish over your paint colors on a scrap piece of wood before painting the table.

The finished table measures about 24" (61 cm) in diameter and about 24½" (62.3 cm) in height.

Tree tables can be designed and painted for a variety of looks. Opposite, the table is painted to resemble an apple tree. Left, the table is painted with tones of peaches and greens.

MATERIALS

- Medium-density fiberboard or MDF, ½" (1.3 cm) thick; one 4' × 8' (1.27 × 2.48 m) sheet is enough for two tables.
- Four ¾" × 15⁄16" (2 × 3.3 cm) desk-top, or figure-8, fasteners with 8 × ½" (1.3 cm) flat-head screws.
- Jigsaw, with blade suitable for dense wood.
- Drill and ⅛" drill bit.
- Sandpaper; mechanical pencil.
- Paintbrush for applying primer and base coat.
- 2" (5 cm) piece of natural sea sponge.

- Primer.
- Latex or acrylic paint for base coat of trunk and foliage areas; two or more accent paints each for trunk and foliage, for sponge paint finish.
- Clear acrylic or polyurethane finish; use marine spar varnish if table will be used outdoors.

CUTTING DIRECTIONS

Cut from the fiberboard two 20" × 24" (51 × 61 cm) rectangles for the base pieces of the table. Cut one 24" (61 cm) square for the table top; set aside.

HOW TO MAKE A TREE TABLE

1 Mark line on base piece 9¾" (25 cm) from one long edge. Position and center the remaining base piece, on its side as shown, aligning the edge with the marked line. Using a mechanical pencil, mark thickness of the board for the cutout slot. Repeat for the remaining base piece.

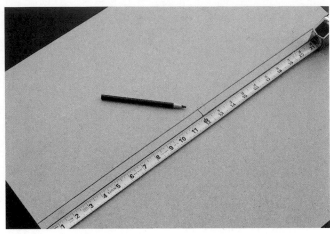

2 Mark a perpendicular line 12⅛" (30.8 cm) from the end of the board for length of cutout slot. Repeat for remaining base piece.

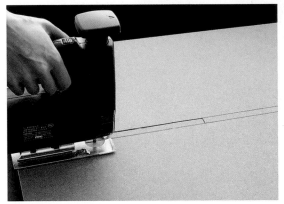

3 Cut, using a jigsaw and following marked line, from edge of board to perpendicular line; at end of cut, keep hand on jigsaw and shut blade off. Remove blade when movement has stopped. Repeat for remaining marked line.

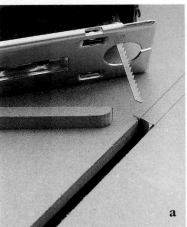

a

b

4 Cut and remove center strip, making curved cut to one corner **(a).** Then trim end of slot even with marked line **(b).** (Marked line was extended for clarity.)

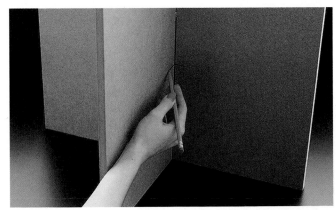

5 Repeat steps 3 and 4 for remaining base piece. Slide pieces together to check fit; mark a registration line as shown, for realigning pieces. Recut or sand the fiberboard as necessary, making sure to match registration line when rechecking fit. Pieces should fit snug but allow some ease for painted finish.

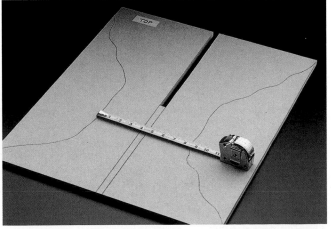

6 Label top of each base piece; cutout slot will be at bottom of one piece and at top of remaining piece. Mark one base piece with design of tree trunk, allowing at least 4" (10 cm) from outer edge of trunk to center of board.

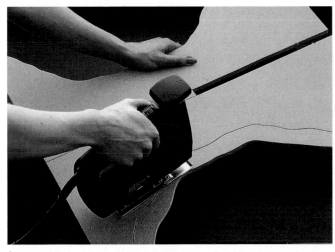

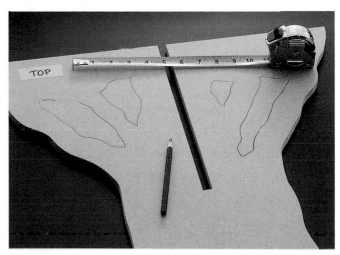

7 Cut about 1½" (3.8 cm) from marked lines to remove bulk of excess board; then recut, following marked lines. Mark and cut remaining base piece, using completed base as a pattern; match top ends of pieces.

8 Mark four cutout areas as shown to create tree branches on upper portion of one base; mark the cutout areas at least 1¾" (4.5 cm) from center slot and 1¼" (3.2 cm) from outside edge of base.

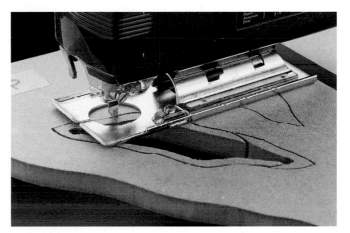

9 Drill a hole slightly larger than jigsaw blade about ¼" (6 mm) in from each end of area to be cut. Insert the jigsaw blade into drilled hole; cut about ¼" (6 mm) from the marked line to opposite drilled hole. Repeat along the opposite edge.

10 Make angled cut to marked line, starting at center area of cutout; cut to center of pointed or curved end. Repeat to cut opposite side. Continue to cut the remainder of cutout.

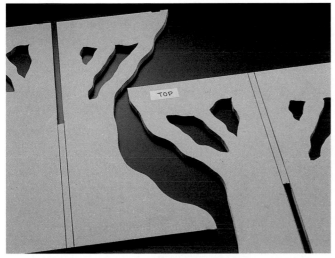

11 Mark cutout areas to create branches for remaining base piece; cut on marked lines.

12 Mark and cut four notches for the desktop fasteners at upper edge of base pieces; position one notch about ¾" (2 cm) from each outside edge. Make the side cuts first; then cut as in step 4, opposite. Wide end of fastener should fit flush in the notch.

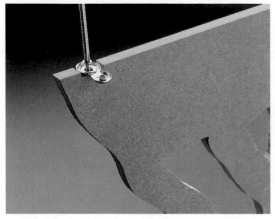

13 Position wide end of fastener, rounded side down, in notch; mark placement for the screw. Predrill, using a ⅛" drill bit; secure fastener. Repeat for remaining fasteners.

14 Mark two perpendicular lines, centered, on underside of tabletop. Mark a line ¼" (6 mm) from each side of the marked lines; outer lines mark placement for table base. Using a straightedge and pencil, mark a circle measuring 12" (30.5 cm) from center point.

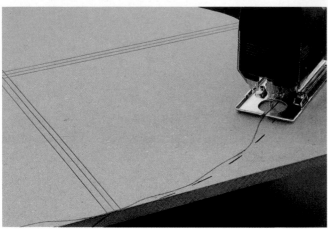

15 Mark a wavy design line for edge of the tabletop, using markings for circle as a guide; cut, following the design line.

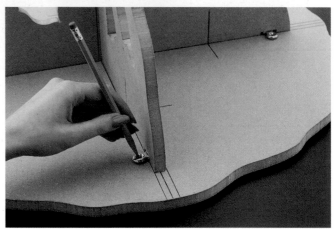

16 Position the table base, upside down, on underside of tabletop, aligning base with marked lines. Mark registration lines for realigning tabletop to base. Mark the placement for screws.

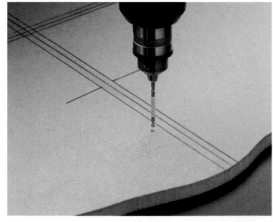

17 Predrill holes for screws on tabletop; to prevent drilling through tabletop, mark ⅜" (1 cm) depth on drill bit, using masking tape; drill until tape reaches surface of board.

18 Secure base to tabletop. Run hand over tabletop at screw locations; if the surface is raised, lightly sand until the surface is flush. Lightly sand the edges of tabletop, base, and cutouts in base. Disassemble the table; apply sponge paint finish (opposite), or paint table as desired.

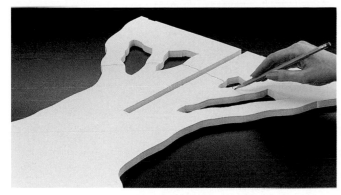

1 Apply primer; allow to dry. Apply second coat to edges of table. Using pencil, lightly mark design lines for lower edge of foliage on base pieces.

2 Apply base coats of paint to table base, using colors of medium value; allow to dry. Using damp natural sponge, dab sponge into darkest paint color for trunk; blot sponge lightly on paper towel. Press sponge repeatedly onto trunk area of table until individual sponge marks cannot be seen; apply more paint to sponge as necessary, blotting on paper towel.

3 Rinse sponge. Allow paint to dry. Apply remaining paint colors to trunk with sponge as in step 2, filling in between previous sponge marks to blend colors.

4 Repeat steps 2 and 3 to sponge paint the foliage on the tabletop and foliage area of base.

5 Apply marine spar varnish, clear acrylic finish, or polyurethane finish, following manufacturer's directions. Allow to dry thoroughly; assemble table.

TWIG WREATHS

Use twigs to create a wreath with a textured, woodsy look. Change the embellishments for each season, using natural items gathered from your yard or walks in the woods. Or for longer-lasting displays, embellish a twig wreath with artificial or preserved foliage. Many embellishments can be simply tucked securely within the twigs, allowing you to use the same wreath year-round. Or make several wreaths, using a variety of twigs.

MATERIALS

- Twigs and small branches; pruning shears.
- Flat wire wreath base.
- 24-gauge paddle floral wire; wire cutter.
- Natural or artificial embellishments, such as pussy-willow stems and silk ivy for spring, artificial fruit and berries for summer, autumn leaves and dried pods for fall, and pine boughs and pinecones for winter.
- Ribbon or raffia, optional.

Spring wreath (opposite), made using birch twigs, features a watering can, seed packets, and artificial vegetables. Sheet moss is tucked between the twigs for additional color.

Autumn wreath (right) is made using branches from a winged euonymus bush. A potted cactus becomes the focal point, and dried chili peppers tucked into the wreath add color.

HOW TO MAKE
A TWIG WREATH

1 Cut twigs into lengths ranging from 10" to 13" (25.5 to 33 cm) long. Bundle several twigs together; wrap with paddle floral wire. Secure paddle floral wire to the wire wreath base. Place twig bundle on base, and tightly wrap with floral wire to secure.

3 Add seasonal embellishments; tuck items between twigs, securing with wire, if necessary.

2 Secure additional twig bundles to base, until entire base is covered; angle bundles so the twigs radiate out in one direction and cover wire of previous bundles.

DECOUPAGE GLASS LUMINARIES

Rose bowl luminaries (above) line a deck rail for a festive look at an outdoor party. A votive, placed in the center of a large bowl, is used as a centerpiece on a buffet table.

Fish bowls (left), attractively embellished with handmade paper, sit on each side of the front door, welcoming guests.

Decorative luminaries can be made from glass containers by gluing pieces of tissue paper to the outside surface. When the candles are lit, the light softly glows through the paper. These luminaries can be made in any size, depending on the size of the container selected.

Colored tissue paper, including matte-finished and pearlized, is available from most card and stationery shops. For a wide color selection, you may want to select paper at an art supply store. Translucent decorative papers can also be used.

To prevent the luminaries from fading, avoid exposing them to direct sunlight.

MATERIALS

- Glass container.
- Tissue paper or translucent decorative paper.
- Decoupage medium; brush or sponge applicator.
- Aerosol acrylic sealer.
- Pillar or votive candle.

HOW TO MAKE DECOUPAGE GLASS LUMINARIES

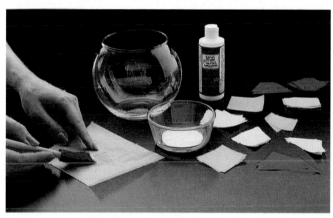

1 Cut the tissue paper into small pieces, varying shapes and sizes as desired. Apply a thin layer of decoupage medium to one piece of paper, using sponge applicator.

2 Position paper on outside of container; gently smooth in place, using finger. Continue applying pieces of paper randomly, overlapping them as desired, until the container is covered. Wrap paper around upper edge of container, to cover rim on inside.

3 Cut decorative motifs, such as geometric shapes or flowers, from paper, if desired, and apply them with decoupage medium.

4 Apply light coat of aerosol acrylic sealer; allow sealer to dry. Apply second coat. Place pillar or votive candle in center of container.

MORE IDEAS FOR LUMINARIES

Sheets of Mylar® (above), wrapped around a votive container, add a shimmery effect.

Minnow buckets (left) become decorative luminaries when illuminated with candles.

Tree branches (above) are drilled and fitted with votive candles for a rustic look. Clamp the log horizontally and drill an opening the depth of the votive, using a spade drill bit. To prevent fire hazard, trim outer layers of bark away from hole.

Sand-filled terra-cotta planters (opposite), filled with pillar candles, illuminate the outdoors. Hurricane pots are made by placing glass chimneys in the sand-filled pots.

INDEX